OECD Reviews on Local Job Creation

Employment and Skills Strategies in England, United Kingdom

This work is published under the responsibility of the Secretary-General of the OECD. The opinions expressed and arguments employed herein do not necessarily reflect the official views of OECD member countries.

This document and any map included herein are without prejudice to the status of or sovereignty over any territory, to the delimitation of international frontiers and boundaries and to the name of any territory, city or area.

Please cite this publication as:
OECD (2015), *Employment and Skills Strategies in England, United Kingdom*, OECD Reviews on Local Job Creation, OECD Publishing, Paris.
http://dx.doi.org/10.1787/9789264228078-en

ISBN 978-92-64-22806-1 (print)
ISBN 978-92-64-22807-8 (PDF)

Series: OECD Reviews on Local Job Creation
ISSN 2311-2328 (print)
ISSN 2311-2336 (online)

The statistical data for Israel are supplied by and under the responsibility of the relevant Israeli authorities. The use of such data by the OECD is without prejudice to the status of the Golan Heights, East Jerusalem and Israeli settlements in the West Bank under the terms of international law.

Photo credits: Cover © Andy Dean Photography/Shutterstock.com; © iStockphoto.com/invictus999.

Corrigenda to OECD publications may be found on line at: *www.oecd.org/about/publishing/corrigenda.htm*.

Preface

Across the OECD, policy-makers are grappling with a critical question: how to create jobs? The recent financial crisis and economic downturn has had serious consequences across most OECD countries, with rising unemployment rates and jobs being lost across many sectors. Indeed, for some countries, the effects the downturn brought with it are continuing, if not amplifying. Shrinking public budgets in some countries also mean that policy makers must now do more with less. In this context, it is necessary to think laterally about how actions in one area, such as employment and training, can have simultaneous benefits in others, such as creating new jobs and better supporting labour market inclusion.

Over recent years, the work of the OECD LEED Programme on *Designing Local Skills Strategies*, *Building Flexibility and Accountability into Local Employment Services*, *Breaking out of Policy Silos*, *Leveraging Training and Skills Development in SMEs* and *Skills for Competitiveness* has demonstrated that local strategies to boost skills and job creation require the participation of many different actors across employment, training, economic development and social welfare portfolios. Employers, unions and the non-profit sector are also key partners in ensuring that education and training programmes provide the skills needed in the labour markets of today and the future.

The *OECD Reviews on Local Job Creation* deliver evidence-based and practical recommendations on how to better support employment and economic development at the local level. This report builds on sub-national data analysis and consultations at the national level and with local stakeholders in two case study areas. It provides a comparative framework to understand the role of the local level in contributing to more and better quality jobs. The report can help national, regional and local policy makers in England build effective and sustainable partnerships at the local level, which join-up efforts and achieve stronger outcomes across employment, training and economic development policies. Co-ordinated policies can help workers find suitable jobs, while also stimulating entrepreneurship and productivity, which increases the quality of life and prosperity within a community as well as throughout the country.

I would like to warmly thank the Department of Business, Innovation and Skills as well as the United Kingdom Commission for Employment and Skills (UKCES) for their active participation and support of the study.

Sergio Arzeni,
Director, OECD Centre for Entrepreneurship, SMEs and Local Development

Acknowledgments

This review has been written by the Local Economic and Employment Development (LEED) Programme of the Organisation for Economic Co-operation and Development (OECD) as part of a project undertaken in co-operation with the UK Commission for Employment and Skills and the Department for Business, Innovation and Skills. This project is part of the OECD LEED programme of work under the leadership of Sylvain Giguère.

Anne Green (University of Warwick) and Steve Johnson (Hull University) have prepared this report under the supervision of Jonathan Barr, Policy Analyst, OECD, who also edited the report. Francesca Froy, Senior Policy Analyst, OECD provided valuable comments. Thanks also go to Michela Meghnagi and Nikolett Kiss for their statistical work and data analysis, as well as Francois Iglesias and other colleagues in the OECD LEED Programme for their assistance with this report.

The authors would also like to acknowledge the valuable contributions of Randall Eberts (Upjohn Institute) for his participation on the project study visit and Carol Oakden, Helen Beck and Lesley Giles (from the UK Commission for Employment and Skills) as well as Gareth Griffiths and Frank Bowley (Department of Business, Innovation and Skills) for their support and inputs during the course of the research.

Finally, special thanks are given to the national and local representatives who participated in the project interviews and roundtables, and provided documentation and comments critical to the production of the report.

Table of contents

Figures

Tables

Boxes

Acronyms and abbreviations

BIS	the Department for Business Innovation and Skills
CPD	continuing professional development
D2N2	Derby, Derbyshire, Nottingham, Nottinghamshire
DCLG	the Department for Communities and Local Government
DfE	the Department for Education
DWP	the Department for Work and Pensions
EFA	Education Funding Agency
EIF	Employer Investment Fund
EMDA	East Midlands Development Agency
EMFEC	East Midlands Further Education Colleges
EOF	Employer Ownership Fund
EOP	Employer Ownership Pilot
ERDF	the European Regional Development Fund
ESB	Employment and Skills Board
ESF	the European Social Fund
ESOL	English for Speakers of Other Languages
FE	Further Education
FJF	Future Jobs Fund
GIF	Growth and Innovation Fund
HE	Higher Education
HEFCE	Higher Education Funding Council for England
HEI	Higher Education institution
HLC	Humber Learning Consortium
HMRC	Her Majesty's Revenue and Customs
IAG	information, advice and guidance
ICT	information and communications technologies
IWP	Innovative Workplaces Project
JCP	Jobcentre Plus

JOT	Job Outcome Target
JSA	Jobseekers Allowance
LAA	Local Area Agreement
LEP	Local Enterprise Partnership
LMI	labour market information
LSSF	Local Support Services Framework
LSP	Local Strategic Partnership
MAC	Migration Advisory Committee
MLP	Mansfield Learning Partnership
NAS	National Apprenticeship Service
NDPB	Non-Departmental Public Body
NEET	not in employment, education or training
NVQ	National Vocational Qualification
OFSTED	Office for Standards in Education Children's Services and Skills
ONS	Office for National Statistics
PES	Public Employment Service
QCF	Qualifications and Credit Framework
RDA	Regional Development Agency
RGF	Regional Growth Fund
SC	Skills Conditionality
SEMTA	Sector Skills Council for Science, Engineering and Manufacturing Technologies
SFA	Skills Funding Agency
SMEs	small and medium-sized enterprises
SSC	Sector Skills Council
SSDA	Sector Skills Development Agency
SSW	Skills Support for the Workforce
STEM	Science, Technology, Engineering, Mathematics
UC	Universal Credit
UK	United Kingdom
UKCES	UK Commission for Employment and Skills
UKWON	United Kingdom Work Organisation Network
ULR	Union Learning Representative
UTC	University Technical College
VET	Vocational education and training

Executive summary

England (and the rest of the UK) was hit hard by the economic crisis, which had a disproportionate impact on certain groups of people and on certain regions. While unemployment did not rise to levels first feared, concerns about worklessness remain – especially among young people and those with poor skills who face particular challenges in building labour market success. The UK economy has returned to sustained but uneven growth, and there are ongoing concerns about the quality of jobs that are available, the rise of more temporary and precarious work and shrinking incomes as pay rises fail to keep up with inflation. Going forward, it is clear that a policy emphasis on the creation of quality jobs will be a key route towards ensuring that everyone can take advantage of a return to economic growth and its associated opportunities.

The OECD Local Economic and Employment Development (LEED) Programme has developed its reviews on Local Job Creation as an international cross-comparative study examining the contribution of local labour market policy to boosting quality employment and productivity. The review in England has focused on local activities in Nottingham and North Nottinghamshire in the East Midlands and in Hull and Scarborough in Yorkshire and the Humber. All local case study areas face particular but inter-connected employment and skills challenges.

England has witnessed important institutional changes in employment, skills and economic development policies in recent years, including the abolition of Regional Development Agencies and the establishment of business-led Local Enterprise Partnerships at the sub-national level. There is a move underway from a centrally-driven system to one of employer ownership of skills, with greater employer and learner input into the design and delivery of the system.

This review has analysed the ability for local employment and training agencies to take a leadership role in developing employment and skills policies. In England, there is a clear trend towards greater flexibilities and decentralisation, especially in large cities. However, the terms and conditions of national regulations and funding policies reduce the ability of local level actors to adjust programmes to local labour market conditions, which differ across England. Partnerships are being used as a key governance tool to bring together the comprehensive range of actors involved in employment, skills and economic development policies. However, the ability to build local strategies is constrained by a lack of clear strategic lead on employment and skills locally, and a lack of autonomy to influence policy at this level.

Education and training opportunities play a critical role in building the supply of skills. While the pool of skilled graduates has expanded through the higher education system, England has long been characterised by a relatively long tail of low skills. As in many other countries, the challenge is how to better connect the education system to the labour market to ensure that the supply of skills being produced is being fully utilised by employers. There has been enhanced emphasis placed on apprenticeship and workplace learning opportunities in the vocational education and training system as "earning while learning" is promoted. The quality of such opportunities needs to be an important priority going forward. There is also a need for more flexible part-time learning options that enable individuals to acquire new skills or strengthen their existing knowledge.

Employer engagement at the local level can help to improve the linkages between the education system and the world of work. The government has recognised this by moving towards a system where businesses have a greater voice in directing and delivering skills development opportunities. However, more needs to be done to better direct young people toward demand occupations through the development of robust local labour market information and career pathways.

Growth and productivity will become increasingly dependent on making better use of the existing skills of the workforce. In some OECD countries (for example the United States, Australia and Flanders), the public sector has taken a leadership role in helping to raise employer ambition, working with employers to upgrade their management and human resources practices so that people are able to contribute fully to the workplace, raising productivity and the jobs on offer at the same time. There is a weak tradition of such activity in England and such work could be expanded, particularly in "low skills equilibrium" regions, such as Hull, where a low supply of skills is matched by a low demand for skills by employers. There is an opportunity to promote and develop policies and programmes which support greater in-work progression, which will produce better quality job opportunities for workers, while stimulating overall productivity and growth within local companies. Local authorities also have an important role to play here in linking the growth agenda with tackling disadvantage and fostering social cohesion.

Partnerships are most likely to be successful when they come together in a spirit of co-operation, encompass informal as well as formal working arrangements and are able to build on a strong base of local information, analytical capacities and intelligence. It is important that the competition for resources created by tendering out of programmes (for example in the field of employment programmes for long term unemployed and for support for hard to reach youth) does not undermine a common purpose and spirit of collaboration locally.

Given concerns about high levels of youth unemployment and potential labour market scarring impacts, policies to tackle disadvantage in England have become increasingly targeted to youth in recent years. Local authorities have traditionally had an oversight role in tackling issues of exclusion and more could be done to ensure that they take a long-term approach to ensuring inclusive growth. Area-based partnerships, which involve the voluntary/community and private sectors, can also play a critical role in promoting employment opportunities for these groups.

Key recommendations

Better aligning programmes and policies to local economic development

- Ensure that local governance structures such as the Local Enterprise Partnerships are "fit for purpose" in terms of the geographical levels at which they operate and the strategic public/private leadership that they engender, while ensuring that they link effectively to national government actors;

- Facilitate the further decentralisation of funding for skills programmes. Review funding arrangements associated with the Skills Funding Agency to allow greater flexibility to meet employer and learner needs at the local level;
- Reinforce the stability of the employment and skills system locally by ensuring that funding and governance arrangements strike an optimal balance between competition and co-operation;
- Ensure that analytical capacity is available at the local level to support data analysis and research capability. This could be through funding of local/sub-regional observatories (perhaps based in universities) or through secondment of statistical and analytical support from central government.

Adding value through skills

- Support schemes to enable SMEs to collaborate on apprenticeship and other types of training while monitoring and evaluating availability and success;
- Fill the gap in careers advice provision by further involving employers in the education system.

Targeting policy to local employment sectors and investing in quality jobs

- Create more and better jobs by supporting key sectors locally and associated skills development initiatives;
- Focus on the benefits of "decent work" and in-work progression by ensuring that public sector organisations "lead by example" and promote the benefits of being a "good employer";
- Develop policies, which encourage the better utilisation of skills and examine the role that Universities and Further Education colleges can play in this area;
- Continue to promote and support entrepreneurship initiatives.

Being inclusive

- Continue to target employment and skills programmes to at-risk youth and other disadvantaged groups to develop their employability skills and better connect them with the labour market. Make greater use of voluntary/community and private sector actors.

Reader's guide

The *Local Job Creation* project involves a series of country reviews in Australia, Belgium (Flanders), Canada (Ontario and Quebec), Czech Republic, France, Ireland, Israel, Italy (Autonomous Province of Trento), Korea, Sweden, the United Kingdom (Northern Ireland and this study of England) and the United States (California and Michigan). The key stages of each review are summarised in Box 1.

Box 1. **Summary of the OECD LEED Local Job Creation Project Methodology**

- Analyse available data to understand the key labour market challenges facing the country in the context of the economic recovery and apply an OECD LEED diagnostic tool which seeks to assess the balance between the supply and demand for skills at the local level
- Map the current policy framework for local job creation in the country
- Apply the local job creation dashboard, developed by the OECD LEED Programme (Froy et al., 2010) to measure the relative strengths and weaknesses of local employment and training agencies to contribute to job creation
- Conduct an OECD study visit, where local and national roundtables with a diverse range of stakeholders are held to discuss the results and refine the findings and recommendations
- Contribute to policy development in the reviewed country by proposing policy options to overcome barriers, illustrated by selected good practice initiatives from other OECD countries

While the economic crisis is the current focus of policy-makers, there is a need for both short-term and longer-term actions to ensure sustainable economic growth. In response to this issue, the OECD LEED Programme has developed a set of thematic areas on which local stakeholders and employment and training agencies can focus to build sustainable growth at the local level. These include:

1. **Better aligning policies and programmes to local economic development challenges and opportunities**;
2. **Adding value through skills**: Creating an adaptable skilled labour force and supporting employment progression and skills upgrading;
3. **Targeting policy to local employment sectors and investing in quality jobs**, including gearing education and training to emerging local growth sectors and responding to global trends, while working with employers on skills utilisation and productivity; and,
4. **Being inclusive** to ensure that all actual and potential members of the labour force can contribute to future economic growth.

Local Job Creation Dashboard

As part of the Local Job Creation project, the LEED Programme has drawn on its previous research to develop a set of best practice priorities in each thematic area, which is used to assess local practice through the local job creation dashboard (see Box 2). The dashboard enables national and local policy-makers to gain a stronger overview of the strengths and weaknesses of the current policy framework, whilst better prioritising future actions and resources. A value between 1 (low) to 5 (high) is assigned to each of the four priority areas corresponding to the relative strengths and weaknesses of local policy approaches based on LEED research and best practices in other OECD countries.

Box 2. **Local Job Creation Dashboard**

Better aligning policies and programmes to local economic development

1.1. Flexibility in the delivery of employment and vocational training policies

1.2. Capacities within employment and VET sectors

1.3. Policy co-ordination, policy integration and co-operation with other sectors

1.4. Evidence based policy making

Adding value through skills

2.1. Flexible training open to all in a broad range of sectors

2.2. Working with employers on training

2.3. Matching people to jobs and facilitating progression

2.4. Joined up approaches to skills

Targeting policy to local employment sectors and investing in quality jobs

3.1. Relevance of provision to important local employment sectors and global trends and challenges

3.2. Working with employers on skills utilisation and productivity

3.3. Promotion of skills for entrepreneurship

3.4. Promoting quality jobs through local economic development

Being inclusive

4.1. Employment and training programmes geared to local "at-risk" groups

4.2. Childcare and family friendly policies to support women's participation in employment

4.3. Tackling youth unemployment

4.4. Openness to immigration

The approach for England

The focus of this study is on the broad range of policies available for job creation, in particular those that are found within employment, skills, education and economic development programmes. Other policies with a more indirect impact are mentioned briefly. The purpose of the study is to describe and evaluate the effectiveness of these policies, in relation to similar policies across the OECD.

The methodology of the study is given by an analytical framework developed by the OECD and applied across a range of countries. This ensures a high level of comparability across the national studies. The framework measures policies in 16 dimensions across four thematic areas. The measurements are based on a set of 100 specific multiple-choice questions. The overall grading has been discussed with local, regional and national stakeholders during three roundtables – of which, two were held in the local case study areas and one at the national level.

In-depth analysis has been undertaken in four local case studies (Nottingham, North Nottinghamshire, Hull and Scarborough) to provide an overall assessment of the English situation. Around 40 interviews were conducted with representatives from local government, the public employment services, Local Enterprise Partnerships, Further Education Colleges, Universities, training providers, careers service providers, business organisations, chambers of commerce, voluntary sector organisations and researchers in each area. These interviews were supplemented by documentary research and email correspondence with other stakeholders, as appropriate.

Following the initial interviews, the OECD conducted a study visit to England in May 2014 to meet with local and national officials to discuss the preliminary results and findings. Following feedback from the visit, the results were supplemented by extra information gathered and points raised in discussion.

Reference

Froy, F., S. Giguère and E. Travkina (2010), *Local Job Creation: Project Methodology*, OECD Local Economic and Employment Development (LEED), www.oecd.org/employment/leed/Local%20Job%20Creation%20Methodology_27%20February.pdf.

Chapter 1

Policy context for employment and skills in England

This chapter provides an overview of England's skills system and the institutional infrastructure and polices for local economic development. The UK economy is heavily services based both in output and employment. In recent decades there has been a marked shift in the UK economy away from manufacturing towards services – particularly towards knowledge intensive services. Historically, national skills policy in England has had a supply-side focus, with the underpinning rationale being to raise skills levels as a means to achieve higher levels of employment, productivity and prosperity. With increasing recognition that a supply-side focus was insufficient, growing policy attention has been placed on stimulating employer demand for skills.

Overview

England is the largest part of the United Kingdom (UK). It is one of the larger member states of the European Union (EU) but is not within the Eurozone. In mid-2013, the population of the UK was estimated at 64.1 million and the population of England at 53.9 million (comprising 84% of the total). Recent growth in population in England is higher than for the UK as a whole and higher than the EU average. There is higher growth of the population in southern England (especially London) than in northern England.

Prior to the recession of 2008-09, the UK economy had been growing rapidly. From 1997-2007, growth averaged 3.2%. During this period, government spending and household consumption became important drivers of domestic growth; while the contribution of net trade declined and private sector debt almost doubled. In 2008 and 2009 the economy suffered its deepest recession since the 1930s and one of the deepest recessions of any major European economy. GDP contracted by 7.2% in real terms between Q1 2008 and Q3 2009. Following 0.8% growth in the first quarter of 2014, GDP attained its pre-recession peak in 2014.

The recent performance of the labour market in the UK compares favourably both to previous recessions and against other economies Between Q2 2008 and Q1 2010, the number of people employed declined by around 2.4% but employment levels have since risen above their pre-recession peak. By mid-2014, 30.64 million people were in employment (the highest level recorded since records began). This represented an employment rate of 73.1% for people aged 16-64 years, which is above the EU average. Yet these aggregate statistics disguise concerns about the number of people on temporary contracts and under-employment (e.g. those working part-time who would prefer to work full-time). Labour productivity remains weak, with output per hour at 4.3 percentage points below its pre-recession peak in Q1 2008. This presents a challenge going forward since there is a danger that those in employment get stuck in low quality jobs without opportunities to gain new skills, earn more and progress in the labour market.

By the spring of 2014, unemployment was 2.12 million: 6.5% of the UK labour force aged 16 years and over could not find a job. The claimant count (i.e. those seeking benefits primarily because they were unable to work) was lower than this. There were 8.78 million economically inactive people (those out of work but not seeking or available to work) aged 16-64. In spring 2014, 817 000 young people aged 16-24 were unemployed, down 141 000 on the previous year. The youth unemployment rate (the proportion of the economically active population who are unemployed) for 16-24 year olds was 17.8%. Despite this improvement, it remains difficult for some young people to secure a first foothold in the labour market and into a fulfilling career.

The UK economy is heavily services based both in output and employment. In recent decades there has been a marked shift in the UK economy away from manufacturing towards services – particularly towards knowledge intensive services; which in 2014 accounted for a third of UK output and over a quarter of total employment. This domination of the service sector – and especially knowledge intensive services – is most pronounced in London and is reflected in an occupational structure skewed towards higher level non-manual occupations (e.g. managerial, professional and associate professional and technical occupations).

Data from the OECD Survey of Adult Skills (e.g. PIAAC) indicates that skills levels in the UK are below the OECD average. In England, adults aged 55-65 perform better than 16-24 year-olds in both literacy and numeracy. In fact, England is the only country where the oldest age group has higher proficiency in both literacy and numeracy than the youngest age group, after other factors, such as gender, socio-economic backgrounds and type of occupations are taken into account (OECD, 2013). In problem solving in technology-rich environments, 42.4% of 16-24 year-olds in England are proficient at Level 2 or 3 compared to the average of 50.7%. Young adults in England scored 21 percentage points lower than those in Korea (the best-performing country) and 4.8 percentage points above young adults in the United States (the lowest performing country). The implication for England is that the stock of skills available to employers is bound to decline over the next decades unless significant action is taken to improve skills proficiency among young people. This could lead to significant skills shortages and a loss of overall competitiveness as business growth is hampered in the future.

Looking at current perceptions of skills demand, the 2013 Employer Skills Survey (conducted by the United Kingdom Commission for Employment and Skills) reveals that 22% of vacancies were considered hard to fill due to a shortage of the necessary skills, which is an increase from 15% in 2011. Vacancies for skilled trades (e.g. mechanics and chefs) were most likely to be considered hard to fill due to a skills shortage (38%), followed by professional roles (29%). Particular concerns have been raised about skills in science, technology, engineering and mathematics (STEM) subjects, which are in demand across many sectors of the economy.

The Government is giving employers more direct control over the design and delivery of training solutions to address skills shortages and improve business performance through a series of investment funds designed to promote employer-led skills solutions, through building the capacity and capability for employers to take ownership of the skills agenda. These include the Employer Ownership Pilot (EOP) and its successor Employer Ownership Fund (EOF) which route public investment directly (on a competitive basis) to employers so that they can design and deliver more flexible training packages. There is also the Growth and Innovation Fund (GIF) which is designed to help employer groups overcome barriers to growth by delivering training to boost innovation and productivity, including through the promotion of workplace practices leading to better development and deployment of workplace knowledge and skills, and the Employer Investment Fund (EIF) which aims to stimulate employer investment in skills and to improve the use of these skills in the workplace.

In international terms the UK has a flexible labour market. The incidence of temporary work is relatively low, average job tenure is also relatively low and the share of part-time employment in total employment is relatively high. A National Minimum Wage was introduced in 1998 and its level relative to the median wage is towards the middle of the range amongst OECD countries. In general terms, institutional structures and approaches may be characterised as market-based, as opposed to being founded on strong social partnership principles as in some parts of continental Europe.

The main central government department with responsibility for labour market and welfare policy is the Department for Work and Pensions (DWP). As outlined further in this report, the public employment service, Jobcentre Plus, is part of the DWP and combines the functions of job broking, referrals to active labour market policy measures and the administration of the benefits system. The Department for Business, Innovation and Skills (BIS) has responsibility for investment in adult skills at Further Education (FE) and Higher Education (HE) levels to promote trade, boost innovation and foster entrepreneurship. It is important to note here that prior to their incorporation as independent bodies in 1992 FE Colleges and Polytechnics were under the control of local authorities. Also of relevance to local partnership working in England is the Department for Communities and Local Government (DCLG) which has a role to create great places to live and work, and to give more power to local people to shape what happens in their area.

DCLG has a vital role in local governance in England, and a key player here is local government. Local government in England is organised on a mixture of one-tier (with unitary authorities) and two-tiered (with district and county authorities) systems. Until recently, there was an increasing trend towards greater central government control of local government, with an overwhelming fiscal reliance on central government funding. The Localism Act 2011 introduced a range of provisions with the aim of empowering and so strengthening the role of local government, including a "general power of competence" allowing local authorities to do anything that an individual may do, other than that which is strictly prohibited. As major employers, local authorities play a key role as anchor institutions in local economies and can play a role in shaping demand through local procurement policies. They also have a role in delivering welfare reform and working with other local partners, through the Local Support Services Framework (LSSF). Since 2011 there has also been provision for local authorities to set up Combined Authorities[1] encompassing two or more local authorities to take on economic development and transport functions.

In November 2014, there were further moves in the direction of greater local flexibility when the Greater Manchester Agreement was announced setting out a devolution agreement between the central government and the Greater Manchester Combined Authority. In the economic development, employment and skills policy domains, this Agreement included the devolution of responsibility for devolved business support budgets, control of the Apprenticeship Grant for Employers in Greater Manchester and power to re-shape and re-structure FE provision. Strengthened governance is a requirement of these new powers; the government expects Greater Manchester to adopt a model of a directly elected city region Mayor. A programme of evaluation of the economic benefits and impacts of new powers is also a requirement of the Agreement. Alongside Greater London, Greater Manchester is at the forefront of devolution in England, reflecting the scale and location of its functional area and the history of local authorities working together. However, there are increasing calls for devolution for other city regions.

Having set out this overview, the following sections of this chapter set out the policy and institutional context for skills and local economic development in England.

Skills policy

From an overtly supply-side focus to increasing recognition of the importance of demand

Historically, national skills policy in England has had a *supply-side focus*, with the underpinning rationale being to raise skills levels as a means to achieve higher levels of employment, productivity and prosperity. Given concerns about a "long tail of low skills in the UK", traditionally, skills policies have focused primarily upon boosting the supply of skills through publicly-funded investments as a route to competitiveness and productivity growth in international terms, as well as social inclusion/mobility.

In this vein, in 2004, the Leitch Review of Skills was tasked with addressing the UK's long-term skill needs. At the end of 2006 Leitch set out a vision and ambitions for the UK to become a "world leader in skills" by 2020, benchmarked in the upper quartile of the OECD (HM Treasury, 2006). This involved targets for enhancing skills attainment at various levels, with the overall aim of shifting upwards the skills profile of the population. The targets were eventually abandoned, but the ambition underlying them remained.

With increasing recognition that a supply-side focus was insufficient, growing policy attention has been placed on *stimulating employer demand for skills*. Indeed, the establishment of employer-led employment and skills boards (ESBs) in some areas (advocated by Leitch) represented a step towards greater involvement of employers in helping shape strategic decisions about training and skills development initiatives to meet local needs. Given that skills are a "derived demand", there has also been increasing recognition of the need for links between business development and skills. In 2002 the Skills for Business framework was established along with 25 Sector Skills Councils (SSCs)[2] led by the Sector Skills Development Agency (SSDA). Following a recommendation of the Leitch Review, the UK Commission for Employment and Skills was established as an executive Non-Departmental Public Body (NDPB), superseding the former SSDA and the National Employment Panel. The UK Commission is constituted as a social partnership ensuring that its strength and influence comes from partnerships formed across business, trade unions, government, industry bodies and education and training organisations. The UK Commission works with government to push forward effective policy with industry to change business behaviour.

Continuity and change in skills policy in England

A useful account of continuity and change in skills policy is provided by Payne and Keep, who highlight how under the UK Labour Government (from 1997 to 2010), skills were foregrounded as a key policy lever to achieve objectives of economic growth and social inclusion in a flexible (deregulated) labour market (Payne and Keep, 2011). While the role of the state was seen as primarily one of helping individuals improve their skills, it was acknowledged that there was a case for intervention where there was assumed to be market failure. Hence, government-funded adult learning was focused mainly around level 2 qualifications (assumed to be the threshold level for employability in the labour market and beneath which individuals were considered to be in "skills poverty") and on a flagship Train to Gain programme providing a subsidy to employers to help employees without such qualifications to gain recognised level 2 (and later level 3) qualifications. During this period, central government also took an increasing role in shaping the direction and management of the education and training system.

Payne and Keep suggested that the skills strategy pursued by the UK Government from 1997 to 2010 rested on three assumptions:

- that a "supply-push" effect would operate – e.g. the belief that increasing the publicly-funded supply of qualified labour would, of itself, enable employers to shift "up-market" and adopt higher value-added, higher productivity, higher skill production strategies;
- that increasing the qualifications of low skilled individuals would allow them to move off welfare, enter employment and progress in the labour market;
- that public subsidy could be used to leverage the additional employer "buy-in" and investment necessary to meet the targets for developing a "world-class" skills base.

Payne and Keep argued that these assumptions were problematic, at least in part, because it may be rational for some employers to pursue low value added skills strategies and also because the low skilled jobs that exist need to be undertaken by someone (Payne and Keep, 2011).

The advent of the UK Conservative-Liberal Democrat Coalition Government in 2010 marked important changes as well as continuities in skills policy. Like the previous Labour Governments, the Coalition Government argued that skills have a crucial role to play in fostering economic competitiveness and social inclusion. But whereas the Labour Government's skills policy involved targets, top-down management of the skills system and important elements of public subsidy, the Coalition Government approach was characterised by a greater role in markets for private investment and smaller government (Payne and Keep, 2011: 27).

The Coalition Government's 2010 Skills Strategy, *Skills for Sustainable Growth,* abolished the Leitch targets and moved beyond "the machinery of central control" as a means to achieve the ambition for world class skills (Department for Business, Innovation and Skills, 2010). The underlying approach of the Coalition Government is voluntaristic and market-based, with an emphasis on learners selecting training and qualifications that are valued by business and which are delivered by a broad range of autonomous training providers attracting learners depending on the quality of their offer.

At the forefront of the Skills Strategy has been expansion and improvements in the numbers of apprenticeships. In terms of paying for the costs of training (other than at basic/ low skills levels for the most disadvantaged groups where public funding will be invested)[3], the main emphasis is on putting responsibility on employers and individuals for ensuring that their own skills needs are met by sharing the costs of training with individuals taking out loans to pay for the costs, as necessary – since they are the beneficiaries of training of a demand-led approach.

The Skills Strategy also acknowledges the importance of raising the profile of employers' demand for skills and ensuring that skills are used to maximum productive effect, so that issues of supply, demand and usage are looked at together. In this vein, the Coalition Government instituted a move away from core grant funding of SSCs, towards competitive funding, strengthening a move towards real employer leadership, co-investment and co-creation, leading to the establishment of new industrial partnerships and employer-led networks.

As part of the broad *employer ownership of skills agenda*, the UK Commission for Employment and Skills has consistently argued that strong employer leadership is the key to tackling skills and productivity challenges, meaning that employers, with their employees, should take greater responsibility for developing skills and jobs for future competitiveness.[4] In late 2011, the Coalition Government announced Employer Ownership Pilots (EOPs), in which businesses were invited to develop new and innovative proposals for tackling the current and future skills needs of their sector, supply chain or local area, in order to test the potential for employer ownership to deliver a competitive skills base.

In the case of successful bids to become EOPs public investment is provided directly to businesses, alongside businesses' own private investment, rather than following the mainstream public funding model where funding is channelled through FE colleges and training providers. Hence, in relation to funding the emphasis has been on use of public money to leverage private money. The overall aim is to find more effective ways to improve skills in the workforce and to use these improved skills to create jobs, drive enterprise and economic growth by seeking co-investment from Government to meet the costs. The direction of travel has been from a complex centrally-driven system to employer ownership of skills through industrial partnerships (involving employers, trades unions and others), designed to create ladders of opportunity, innovation and growth aligned with industrial strategy and local priorities.

Institutional structures and funding for local economic growth[5]

Changing institutional structures and initiatives for local economic growth

Addressing sub-national variations in economic growth has been a longstanding focus of central government policy in the UK, but structures and funding initiatives have often been replaced by new schemes. Analysis by the National Audit Office identifies 38 regional and local initiatives (e.g. schemes/bodies) over the period from 1975-2013 with the pace of change being particular rapid over the period since the late 1990s (National Audit Office, 2013). 24 regional and local initiatives have been introduced during the period from the late 1990s to 2013, of which 10 remained operational at the end of 2013. This highlights the regularity of change. A change in the UK Government in May 2010 heralded important changes in policy mechanisms, initiatives and governance structures, alongside new local freedoms and responsibilities.

The rise and demise of the regional tier of governance

Following the establishment of Government Offices for the Regions by the previous UK Conservative Government in 1994, when in office from 1997-2010, successive UK Labour Governments strengthened the tier of regional governance in England. Eight Regional Development Agencies (RDAs) were launched in 1999 covering each of the regions of England outside London, and a ninth RDA for London was established in 2000. The RDAs had five statutory purposes:

- to further economic development and regeneration;
- to promote business efficiency, investment and competitiveness;
- to promote employment;
- to enhance development and application of skills relevant to employment; and
- to contribute to sustainable development.

In practice, RDAs' responsibilities encompassed regeneration, competitiveness, inward investment, as well as regional partnerships and skills. RDAs' activities in relation to skills strengthened over time, with the establishment of Regional Skills Partnerships, offering a forum for employers, learning and skills providers and other public bodies to establish regional skills priorities and collectively influence how the delivery of skills could best provide support for regional businesses and deliver RDAs' Regional Economic Strategies. In 2009 the strategic skills function of RDAs was strengthened, with each RDA being charged with responsibility for producing a Regional Skills Strategy as a core element of a new integrated Regional Strategy. The Regional Skills Strategies involved the RDAs working in partnership with the SSCs, local authority leaders and sub-regional bodies to produce strategies articulating employer demand and more closely aligning skills priorities with economic development.

The UK Coalition Government made a formal announcement of its intention to abolish RDAs shortly after taking office in May 2010. Closure of RDAs was finalised in 2012, but in practice the activities of RDAs contracted immediately and staff left and the activities of RDAs were curtailed from the latter part of 2010 onwards. Some responsibilities of RDAs were passed upwards to the national tier and some were passed to the local tier to newly-established Local Enterprise Partnerships (LEPs). However, while the transfer of powers upwards to central government departments proceeded as planned, the transfer of responsibility downwards to the local level occurred gradually over a different time frame, in a relatively uncoordinated way.

The tenets of local economic growth policy from 2010

The UK Coalition Government set out its approach to local economic growth in the White Paper *Local growth: realising every place's potential*, based on three main principles reflecting the localism agenda (i.e. to devolve power to communities) (HM Government, 2010):

- to shift powers to local communities and businesses – principally through the closure of the RDAs and the introduction of Local Enterprise Partnerships (LEPs);
- to promote efficient and dynamic markets and increase confidence to invest: through reforms to the planning system and the introduction of new incentives and powers for local authorities such as the New Homes Bonus, business rates retention and tax increment financing; and
- focused investment – initially through the Regional Growth Fund and subsequently through the Growing Places Fund, Enterprise Zones and City Deals (as outlined further below).

Local Enterprise Partnerships (LEPs)

The Coalition Government's proposals for LEPs in England were set out in June 2010 in a joint letter from Secretaries of State at the Department for Communities and Local Government (DCLG) and the Department for Business, Innovation and Skills (BIS) to local councils and business leaders. The letter invited local consortia to submit proposals for partnerships with local business and civic leaders, operating in local areas making economic sense, to provide the vision, knowledge and strategic leadership to set local economic priorities. At the time of writing in 2014, there are 39 LEPs in England, comprising groupings of local authority areas, with some local authorities having membership of two LEP areas (e.g. some LEP areas overlap). The first 24 LEPs were announced in October 2010 and the final LEP was approved by central government in December 2011. This illustrates that some LEPs were formally established and operational before others.

LEPs are strategic non-statutory bodies, with delivery implemented through partners. Roles set out for LEPs in the Local Growth White Paper included:

- working with Government to set out key investment priorities, including transport infrastructure and co-ordinating and supporting policy delivery;
- co-ordinating proposals or bidding directly for the Regional Growth Fund (see below);
- supporting high growth businesses by bringing together and supporting consortia to run new growth hubs;
- co-ordinating approaches to leveraging funding from the private sector;
- supporting the transition to the low carbon economy; and
- working with local employers, Jobcentre Plus (i.e. the Public Employment Service) and learning providers to help local workless people into jobs.

To some extent the role set out for LEPs in the Local Growth White Paper suggests that their contribution might be seen in the so-called "soft spaces" of local economic development, where they might exert influence and help build partnerships, networks and institutional capacity (Haughton and Allmendinger, 2008).

In practice, the role of LEPs has expanded over time. By 2014, they had responsibility for the Growing Places Fund and Enterprise Zones. Following a recommendation in the Heseltine Report *No Stone Unturned: In Pursuit of Growth* for a greater devolution of funding from central government to LEPs in order that government investment in economic development could be tailored directly to the individual challenges and opportunities of local communities and could be augmented by private sector investment, central government began the process of setting up Growth Deals with LEPs to operate from 2015-16 (Haseltine, 2012). These Growth Deals include the Local Growth Fund through which funding for skills, housing and transport will be distributed through a mix of allocation and competition, based on LEPs' Strategic Economic Plans (SEPs) which were submitted to government at the end of March 2014. The first wave of Growth Deals was announced in July 2014.[6] In 2014, LEPs will assume responsibility for delivering part of the EU Structural and Investment Funds to 2020.

Overall, the progress of LEPs across England has varied, but in general has been affected by limited resources and capacity, coupled with taking on more responsibilities, at a time when local authorities (who are key partners) have seen their budgets declining.

Enterprise Zones

The Government announced new Enterprise Zones in the 2011 Budget, and these have been operational since 2012.[7] Enterprise Zones are geographically-defined areas hosted by LEPs in which businesses can receive a range of incentives to start up or expand – including simplified planning; a short-term discount on business rates; and government support to provide superfast broadband. The rationale is that Enterprise Zones help LEPs to attract investment and jobs. Hence, rather than having locations at the heart of the most deprived communities, Enterprise Zones are located in areas where there is potential for growth. In 2014, there are 24 Enterprise Zones in England.[8]

Funding for local economic growth in England in 2014

This section sets out the main funding streams for local economic growth operational in England at the time when local roundtables were conducted in May 2014.

The Growing Places Fund

The Growing Places Fund was announced in 2011. It is overseen by LEPs and is designed to tackle immediate infrastructure investment constraints, with a focus on housing and transport.

The Regional Growth Fund

The Regional Growth Fund (RGF) was announced in 2010. It is intended to help areas and communities at risk of being particularly affected by public spending cuts (i.e. those with a relatively high dependence on public sector employment), by encouraging private sector enterprise and levering private sector investment. Funding is allocated on a competitive basis. LEPs and local authorities were eligible to apply for funding from the first four funding rounds, with subsequent rounds focused exclusively on private enterprises.

City Deals

City Deals are agreements between central government and cities that aim to give new powers, freedoms and funding mechanisms to local decision-makers in exchange for greater responsibility for stimulating and supporting economic growth in their area.[9] Skills development is one element in City Deals. The first wave of deals was with the Core Cities (i.e. the eight largest cities[10] in England outside London). The government agreed to the first wave of eight City Deals in July 2012. The second wave of City Deals involved 20 cities (the next 14 largest cities outside of London and their wider areas[11] and the six cities with the highest population growth from 2001 to 2010).

Other funds

The funds outlined above are set within other ongoing spending supporting economic growth, including by local authorities, central government and European funding streams.

Funding reductions

In line with plans for deficit reduction, there has been reduced spending for local growth programmes in recent years. Over the five-year period from 2010-11 to 2014-15 the government is due to spend a total of GBP 6.2 billion on local growth programmes, compared with GBP 11.2 billion spent by RDAs over the five-year period from 2005-06 to 2009-10 (National Audit Office, 2013).[12]

Summary

Over the medium-term there have been continuities and changes in skills policy in England. There has been increasing recognition of the importance of focusing on stimulating employers' demand for skills and having employers play a greater role in shaping training and skills development policies.

The thrust of skills and local economic growth policy has been towards greater devolution of powers to the local level. Ahead of the May 2015 UK General Election, the Labour Party has announced plans for greater devolution of powers from Whitehall (i.e. central government), including over skills policy to more powerful city-regions.

Regular change is a key feature of the institutional architecture in England for employment and skills and for local economic growth. However, the period since 2010 has been one of particularly intense change as old structures have been abolished and new ones have been created. For part of this period there was a hiatus as old structures were dismantled before new ones became established and/or found a role for themselves.

There have also been cuts in public spending in fields related to skills and local economic development. This has both stimulated competition for available funds and fostered continuation of local partnership working (albeit the identity of some of the partners has changed with organisational changes). Complexity and change of the nature and scale that has been seen in England in recent years has the potential to increase confusion and stifle sub-national partnership working, making it difficult for policy makers, employers and individuals to know where best or how best to engage. This is of critical importance, especially given the voluntaristic emphasis of skills policy and the trends towards greater local devolution.

Notes

1. On 1 April 2014 there were Combined Authorities in Greater Manchester, West Yorkshire, South Yorkshire (Sheffield) and Liverpool.

2. Independent, employer led UK-wide organisations focusing on certain industrial sectors which aim to develop high quality skills standards with employers to support productivity and profitability growth and enhance competitiveness.

3. People in England who are unemployed, claiming benefit and whose lack of skills is a barrier to finding work are eligible for training that is fully funded by central government.

4. For a policy statement on this policy theme see: https://www.gov.uk/government/publications/growth-through-people-a-statement-on-skills-in-the-uk (accessed 21 July 2014).

5. Note that, unless otherwise stated, the initiatives, funds and structures described in this section apply to England only. The devolved governments of Scotland, Wales and Northern Ireland have some powers to develop and implement their own local and regional economic development and skills policies.

6. See https://www.gov.uk/government/news/growth-deals-firing-up-local-economies (accessed 21 July 2014).

7. There had been Enterprise Zones previously.

8. Locations include Nottingham and Hull.

9. Operationally the cities involved in City Deals negotiate deals with government with the help of the Cities Policy Unit. The Cities Policy Unit was created in August 2011. It is made up of civil servants and staff seconded from local government, think tanks and the private sector. It works jointly with the Department for Business Innovation and Skills and the Department for Communities and Local Government and across Whitehall (i.e. central government departments).

10. Nottingham is one of these cities. The Core Cities Group has subsequently been expanded to include Cardiff (Wales) and Glasgow (Scotland).

11. Hull and the Humber is included in Wave 2 of City Deals.

12. For further details on the expenditure on specific local growth programmes by financial year see Appendix 3 in National Audit Office (2013).

References

Department for Business, Innovation and Skills (2010), Skills for Sustainable Growth, BIS, London, https://www.gov.uk/government/uploads/system/uploads/attachment_data/file/31506/10-1285-skills-for-sustainable-growth-summary-responses.pdf (accessed 21 July 2014).

Haughton, G. and P. Allmendinger (2008), "The soft spaces of local economic development", *Local Economy*, 23 (2), 138-148.

Heseltine, M. (2012), *No Stone Unturned in pursuit of Growth*, Department for Business Innovation and Skills, London.

HM Government (2010), *Local Growth: Realising Every Place's Potential*, Department for Business Innovation and Skills, London.

HM Treasury (2006), *Leitch Review of Skills: Prosperity for all in the global economy – world class skills*, The Stationery Office, London.

Leitch, S. (2006), *Prosperity for All in the Global Economy – World Class Skills*, Final report of the Leitch Review of Skills, HMSO/HM Treasury, London.

National Audit Office (2013), *Funding and structures for local economic growth*, The Stationery Office, London.

OECD (2013), *OECD Skills Outlook 2013: First Results from the Survey of Adult Skills*, OECD Publishing, Paris, http://dx.doi.org/10.1787/9789264204256-en.

Payne, J. and E. Keep (2011), "One Step Forward, Two Steps Back? Skills Policy in England under the Coalition Government", *SKOPE Research Paper* 102, Cardiff and Oxford Universities.

UKCES (2012), *UK Commission's Employer Skills Survey 2013: UK results*, https://www.gov.uk/government/uploads/system/uploads/attachment_data/file/327492/evidence-report-81-ukces-employer-skills-survey-13-full-report-final.pdf (accessed 21 July 2014).

Chapter 2

Overview of the English case study areas

To better understand the role of the local level in contributing to job creation and productivity, this review examined local activities in four areas in England – two from each of two regions: (1) *Nottingham; and* (2) *North Nottinghamshire; (from the East Midlands); and* (3) *Hull; and* (4) *Scarborough; (from Yorkshire and the Humber). This chapter provides a labour market and economic overview of each area as well as the results from an OECD LEED statistical tool which looks at the relationship between skills supply and demand at the sub-national level.*

Overview of the local case study areas

The local case studies for England were selected to represent a variety of positions on local skills supply and demand indicators (see subsequent discussion) and of local economic, employment and governance conditions. Two case study areas are located in the East Midlands: Nottingham and North Nottinghamshire. Two are located in Yorkshire and the Humber: Hull and Scarborough.

Nottingham

Nottingham is a "core city" (e.g. a major regional city) in England and it has an urban area of 310 800 people for which Nottingham City Council has administrative responsibility. The Nottingham City NUTS 3 area is classified as having a "skills surplus" (see further discussion later in the chapter) but the geographically surrounding area of South Nottinghamshire (comprising the lower tier local authority areas of Broxtowe, Gedling and Rushcliffe which have strong functional links to Nottingham City) is a "high skills equilibrium" area.

Nottingham has two universities and two Further Education Colleges. Nottingham City has an Enterprise Zone; a City Deal (with associated plans for apprenticeships, retention of graduates and investment in high tech firms). It had an early Employment and Skills Board which was in existence for longer than any other ESB in England. It was a City Strategy Pathfinder from 2007 to 2011 with a range of initiatives focused on inclusion and skills development for workless people. It is part of the larger D2N2 (Derby and Derbyshire, Nottingham and Nottinghamshire) LEP area (see Figure 2.1).[1]

Figure 2.1. **Map of the D2N2 LEP area**

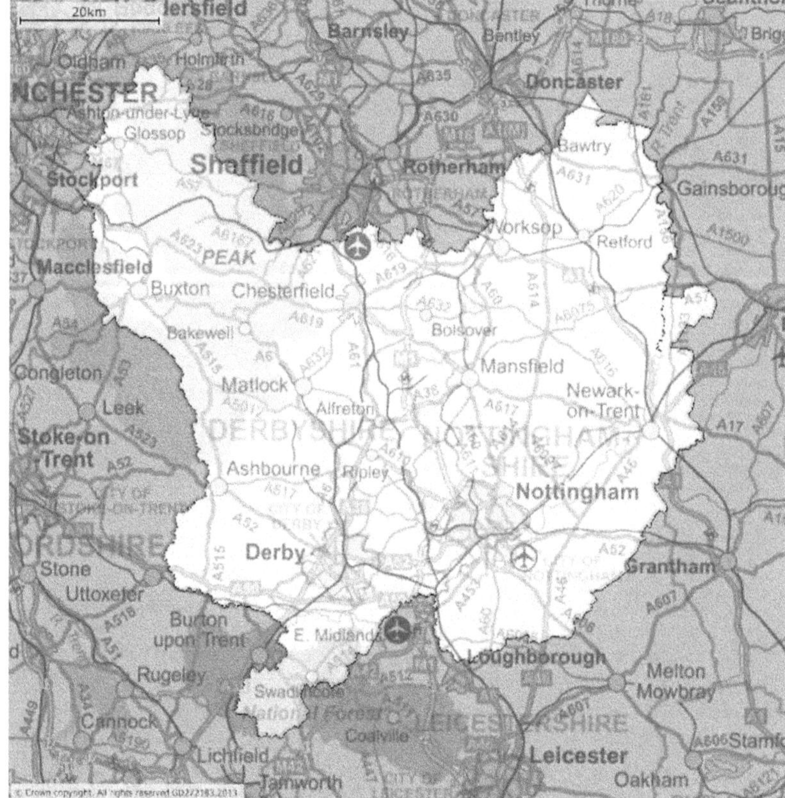

North Nottinghamshire

North Nottinghamshire is classified as a "rural" area (albeit it includes some substantial urban areas), which comprises the lower tier local authority areas of Ashfield, Bassetlaw, Mansfield, and Newark and Sherwood (which together with the lower tier local authority areas in South Nottinghamshire form part of Nottinghamshire County Council).

Along with neighbouring parts of North East Derbyshire, it is an ex-coal mining area where many jobs in mining (taken by men) and in textiles (predominantly taken by women) have been lost in recent decades. Some parts of the area have good accessibility close to the M1 motorway but some residents face issues of physical accessibility to jobs which compound their employment challenges. This area has also been identified as one where there is a concentration of in-work poverty. It does not have access to a City Deal. North Nottinghamshire is part of the larger D2N2 (Derby and Derbyshire, Nottingham and Nottinghamshire) LEP area. Bassetlaw District in North Nottinghamshire is also part of the Sheffield City Region LEP to the north.

Hull

Hull is an urban area in the eastern part of Yorkshire and the Humber located on the "North Bank" of the Humber estuary. As such, it is a relatively peripheral city (in terms of the geography of England). The city had a population of 257 600 in 2013, for which Hull City Council (an upper tier local authority) has administrative responsibility. Hull has a history of relatively poor performance on economic and social indicators. It is in Wave 2 of the City Deals and is part of The Humber LEP (see Figure 2.2) and has one University,

Figure 2.2. **Map of the Humber LEP area**

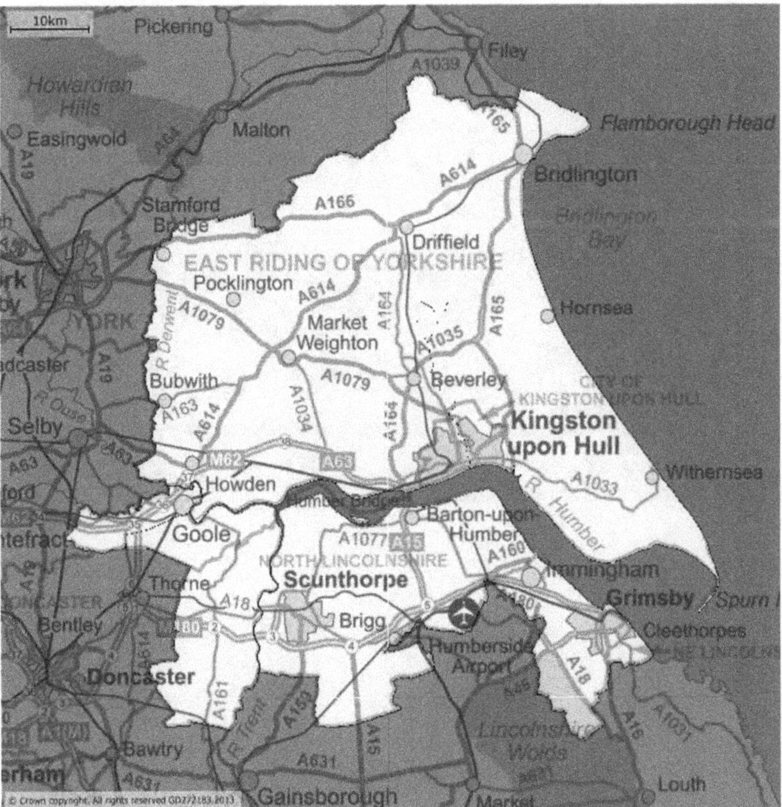

two large FE colleges and a number of other education and VET providers, some located outside of the city boundary but within daily travelling distance.

Scarborough

Scarborough is a seaside town on the Yorkshire coast (north of Hull). Scarborough district (a lower tier local authority area) had a population of 108 200 in 2013. Scarborough is one small part of the geographically very expansive North Yorkshire NUTS 3 area and falls within the York, North Yorkshire and East Riding LEP (see Figure 2.3), covering north and east Yorkshire. Being in a small District within a largely rural county, Scarborough has had limited access to City Deals and other programmes to decentralise economic development funding, so on balance has had less local flexibility than has been the case for Hull. There are two FE colleges located within the Scarborough District boundary and the University of Hull operates a campus in the town.

Figure 2.3. **York, North Yorkshire and East Riding LEP area**

A map showing all LEP areas in England is presented in Figure 2.4, with districts that fall within overlapping LEP areas identified.

Figure 2.4. **LEP areas in England**

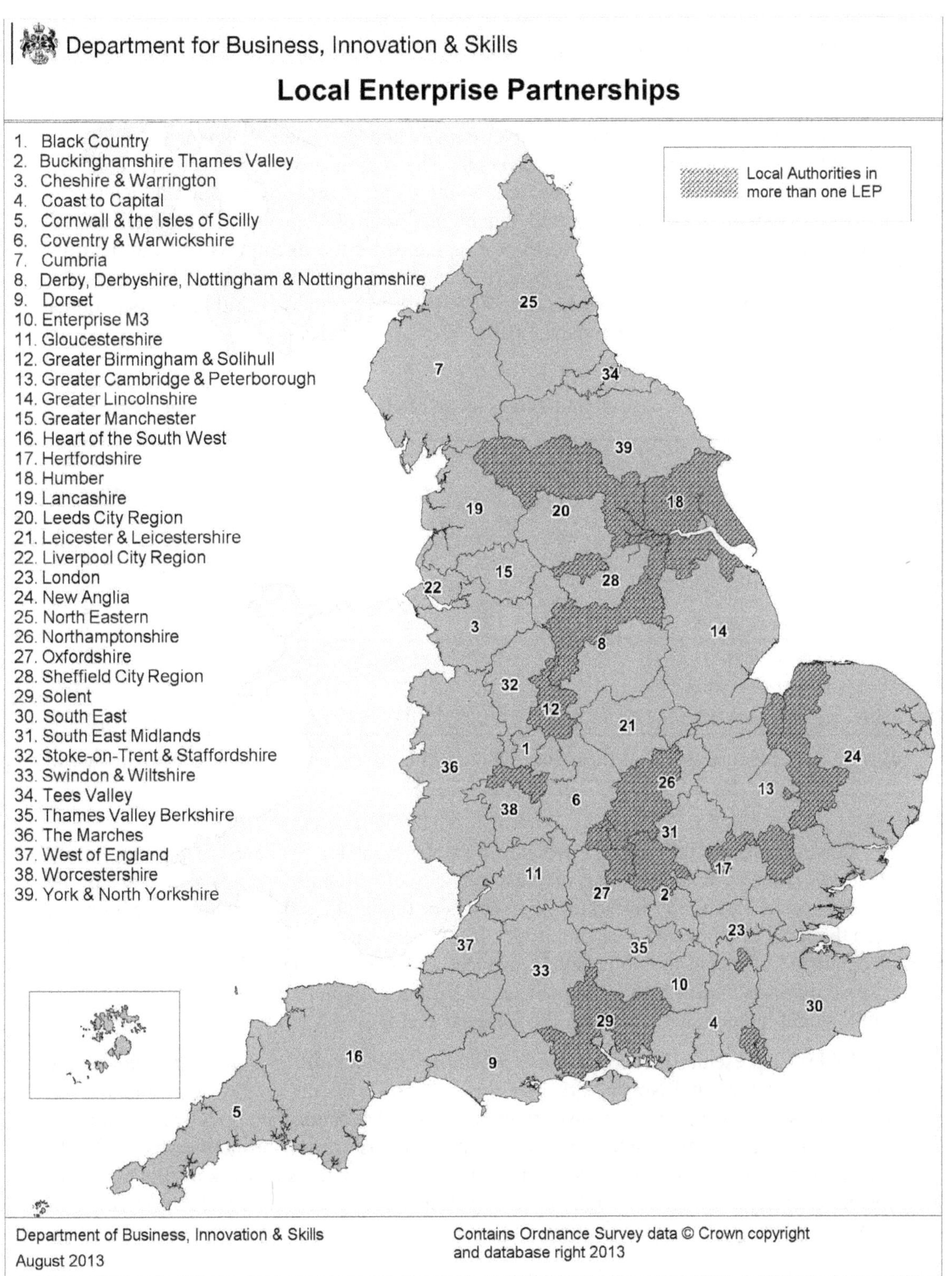

Key features on economic position and employment profile indicators

This section presents a snapshot of key characteristics of the local case study areas relative to functionally related local areas and England on selected economic position and profile indicators using residence-based information from the 2014 Annual Population Survey.

Table 2.1 shows that Nottingham and Hull had substantially lower employment rates for people of working age than the England average, while neighbouring districts (South Nottinghamshire and the East Riding of Yorkshire, respectively) displayed rates slightly higher than the UK average. Likewise in Nottingham and Hull unemployment and economic inactivity rates exceeded the England average. The presence of relatively large numbers of students in further and higher education is one factor depressing the employment rates in the cities, while both also contain neighbourhoods of deprivation characterised by high levels of unemployment. In North Nottinghamshire the unemployment rate and the percentage of working age people who were economically inactive were slightly above the England average and the employment rate slightly lower. North Yorkshire displays a higher employment rate than the England average.

Table 2.1. **Economic position indicators for selected TL3 regions in England, 2013**

Economic position	North Nottinghamshire	Nottingham	South Nottinghamshire	Hull	East Riding of Yorkshire	North Yorkshire	ENGLAND
Employment rate (16-64)	70.2	60.3	72.8	63.3	74.9	74.7	71.9
Unemployment rate (16 and over)	7.9	11.7	7.2	13.9	6.1	4.8	7.1
% who are economically inactive (16-64)	23.6	31.6	21.6	26.3	20.1	21.3	22.5

Source: Annual Population Survey (March-May 2014), Office for National Statistics (ONS), https://www.nomisweb.co.uk/query/select/getdatasetbytheme.asp?theme=28.

Table 2.2 shows the sectoral profile of employment for residents in the case study areas. As is the case for England, the vast majority of residents in employment are in the service sector, albeit only in Nottingham (a major regional centre for the East Midlands) does the share of employed residents in services exceed the average for England. The share of employed residents in public sector services exceeds the England average in all local case study areas. North Nottinghamshire and Hull are characterised by a greater share of employment in manufacturing than the England average.

Table 2.3 presents the occupational profile of residents in employment. Outside the rural areas of East and North Yorkshire the share of residents employed in managerial and professional occupations is lower than the England average. The under-representation relative to higher-level non-manual occupations is most pronounced in North Nottinghamshire. 28% of residents are in elementary occupations or work as process, plant and machine operatives. Nottingham and Hull also have shares of residents working in elementary occupations that are above the England average.

Table 2.2. **Sectoral profile of residents in employment in selected TL3 regions in England, 2013**

Sectoral profile of employment (%)	North Nottinghamshire	Nottingham	South Nottinghamshire	Hull	East Riding of Yorkshire	North Yorkshire	ENGLAND
A: Agriculture and fishing	1.1	!	!	1.6	3.2	3.8	0.9
B,D,E: Energy and water	3.2	1.2	3.1	2.4	1.4	1.5	1.5
C: Manufacturing	14.2	8.8	11.6	14.0	13.7	11.0	9.6
F: Construction	8.3	6.9	8.7	8.5	5.7	7.8	7.3
G,I: Distribution, hotels and restaurants	17.2	20.5	17.7	22.2	19.3	18.1	18.4
H,J: Transport and communications	8.4	9.1	7.9	7.3	6.5	6.7	9.2
K-N: Banking, finance and insurance	10.6	14.1	13.5	9.1	10.5	16.1	17.2
O-Q: Public admin. education and health	32.4	33.3	33.1	29.8	33.3	29.8	29.5
R-U: Other services	4.2	4.6	3.5	4.3	5.5	5.0	5.6
G-Q:Total services	72.7	81.6	75.6	72.7	75.2	75.7	79.8

Note: ! estimate not available
Source: Annual Population Survey (March-May 2014), Office for National Statistics (ONS), https://www.nomisweb.co.uk/query/select/getdatasetbytheme.asp?theme=28.

Table 2.3. **Occupational profile of residents in employment in selected TL3 regions in England, 2013**

Occupational profile of employment (%)	North Nottinghamshire	Nottingham	South Nottinghamshire	Hull	East Riding of Yorkshire	North Yorkshire	ENGLAND
1: Managers, directors and senior officials	6.1	5.2	9.3	6.7	12.3	14.0	10.5
2: professional occupations	13.4	18.4	28.8	14.0	17.9	20.8	19.9
3: associate prof & tech occupations	12.1	11.9	13.3	10.2	13.2	12.4	14.3
4: administrative and secretarial occupations	12.3	9.8	10.1	8.9	10.2	10.6	10.7
5: skilled trades occupations	12.8	8.5	9.3	13.1	10.7	14.1	10.4
6: caring, leisure and other service occupations	8.8	8.6	8.7	9.8	10.2	7.1	9.0
7: sales and customer service occupations	6.1	10.5	7.5	11.2	8.0	6.9	7.8
8: process, plant and machine operatives	13.2	8.4	5.4	10.9	6.0	5.7	6.2
9: elementary occupations	14.7	17.4	6.8	14.5	10.8	8.4	10.6

Source: Annual Population Survey (March-May 2014), Office for National Statistics (ONS), https://www.nomisweb.co.uk/query/select/getdatasetbytheme.asp?theme=28.

Balance between skills supply and demand at the sub-national level

The LEED Programme has developed a statistical tool to understand the balance between skills supply and demand within local labour markets (Froy, Giguère and Meghnagi, 2012). In the English context, this tool can help to provide policy makers with an understanding of skills mismatches, which may occur at the sub-national level. It can inform place-based policy approaches at the local level.

Looking at Figure 2.5, in the top-left corner (skills gaps and shortages), the supply of high skills is insufficient to meet demand for such skills, a situation that results in reported skills gaps and shortages. In the top-right corner, demand for high skills is met by an equal supply of high skills, resulting in a high-skill equilibrium. This is the most desired

Figure 2.5. **Understanding the relationship between skills supply and demand**

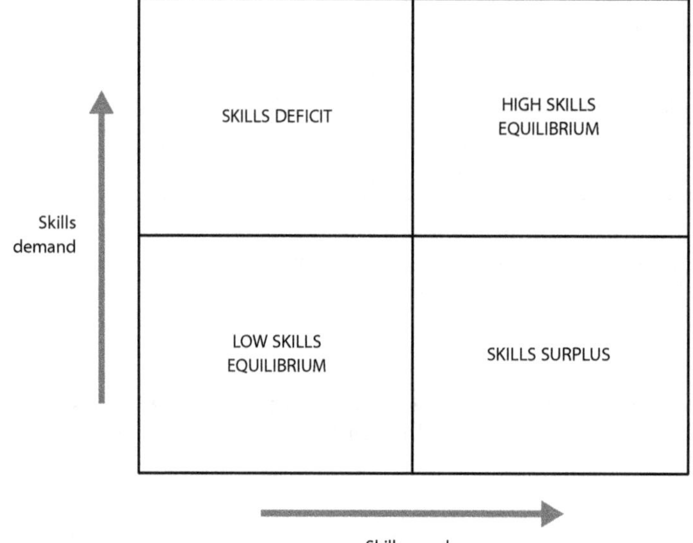

Source: Froy, F. and S. Giguère (2010), *Putting in Place Jobs that Last: A Guide to Rebuilding Quality Employment at Local Level*, OECD Local Economic and Employment Development (LEED) Working Papers, No. 2010/13, OECD Publishing, Paris, http://dx.doi.org/10.1787/5km7jf7qtk9p-en.

Box 2.1. **Explaining the diagnostic tool**

The analysis is carried out at Territorial Level 3 regions (regions with populations ranging between 150 000 and 800 000). The supply of skills was measured by the percentage of the population with post-secondary education. The demand for skills was measured by the percentage of the population employed in medium-high skilled occupations. Regions are also classified in relation to the average state unemployment rate. The indices are standardised using the inter-decile method and are compared with the national median. Further explanations on the methodology can be found in Froy, Giguère and Meghnagi, 2012.

Source: Froy, F., S. Giguère and M. Meghnagi (2012), *Skills for Competitiveness: A Synthesis Report*, OECD Local Economic and Employment Development (LEED) Working Papers, No. 2012/09, OECD Publishing, Paris, http://dx.doi.org/10.1787/5k98xwskmvr6-en.

destination of all high performing local economies. In the bottom-left corner the supply of and demand for low skills meet resulting in a low-skill equilibrium. The challenge facing policymakers is to get the economy moving towards the top-right corner. Lastly, in the bottom-right corner, demand for low skills is met by a supply of high skills resulting in an economy where not all high skills are available are not utilised. This can lead to the out migration of talent, underemployment, skill under-utilisation and attrition of human capital, all of which signal missed opportunities for creating prosperity.

This typology was applied to English regions, including the local case study areas of Nottingham and North Nottinghamshire in the East Midlands and Hull and North Yorkshire (including Scarborough) in Yorkshire and the Humber – see Figures 2.6 and 2.7.

Figure 2.6. **Balancing skills supply and demand in the East Midlands, 2011**

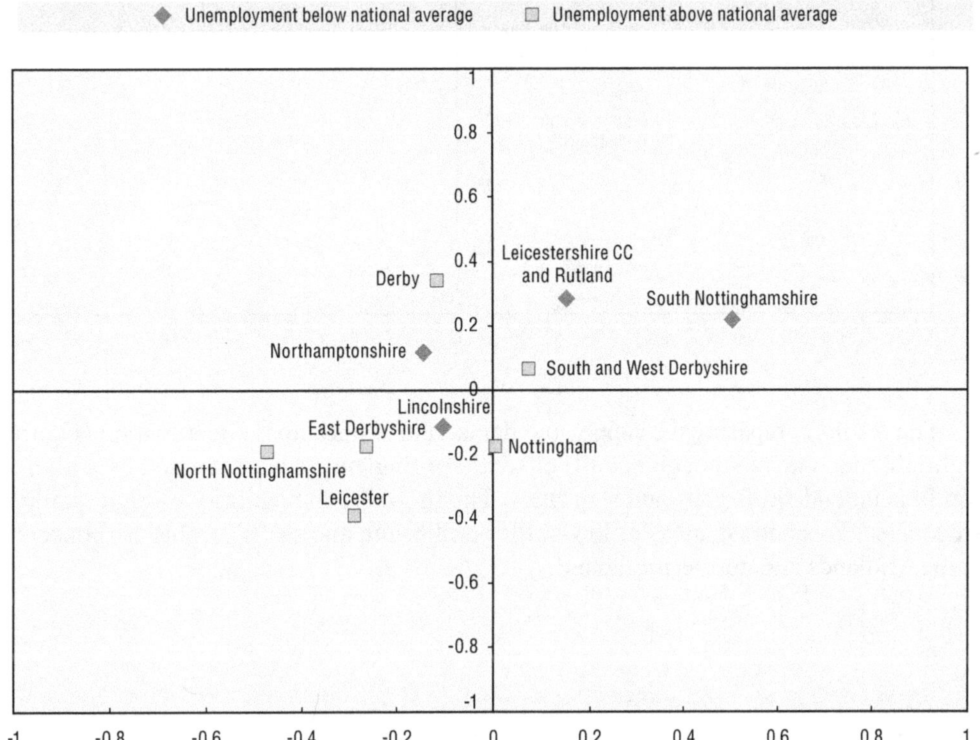

The results from this analysis show variations across the regions. North Nottinghamshire falls into the low-skills equilibrium quadrant, demonstrating the conjunction of low supply and demand for skills. Nottingham has a higher than average unemployment rate and falls into the "skills surplus" quadrant, suggesting that there is a relatively low demand for skills relative to supply. However, the South Nottinghamshire with which it is linked, along with the nearby South and West Derbyshire area are located in the high-skills equilibrium quadrant. Derby is also characterised by a relatively high demand for skills.

Hull is a tightly bounded NUTS 3 area and is characterised by a low-skills equilibrium, as are the areas on the South Bank of the Humber (see Figure 2.7). However, the East Riding of Yorkshire which is adjacent to Hull is in the high-skills equilibrium quadrant. The North Riding of Yorkshire (in which Scarborough is located) falls just into the skills gaps and shortages quadrant, but it is likely that Scarborough shares many of the characteristics of a low-skills equilibrium.

Figure 2.7. **Balancing skills supply and demand in Yorkshire and the Humber, 2011**

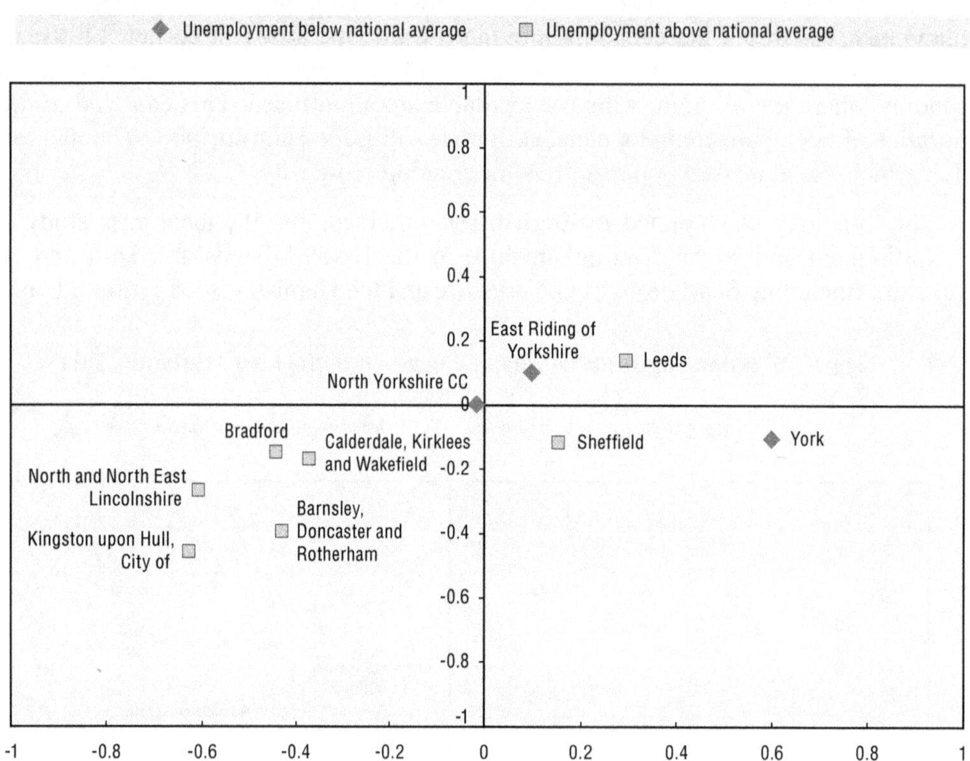

The results comparing the supply and demand of skills across Great Britain (Figure 2.8) highlight that much (although not all) of southern England is characterised by a high-skills equilibrium and skills gaps and shortages. This is where the majority of high quality jobs are located. By contrast, areas of low-skills equilibrium and skills surplus are concentrated in the Midlands and northern England.

Figure 2.8. **Skills supply and demand, 2011, United Kingdom**

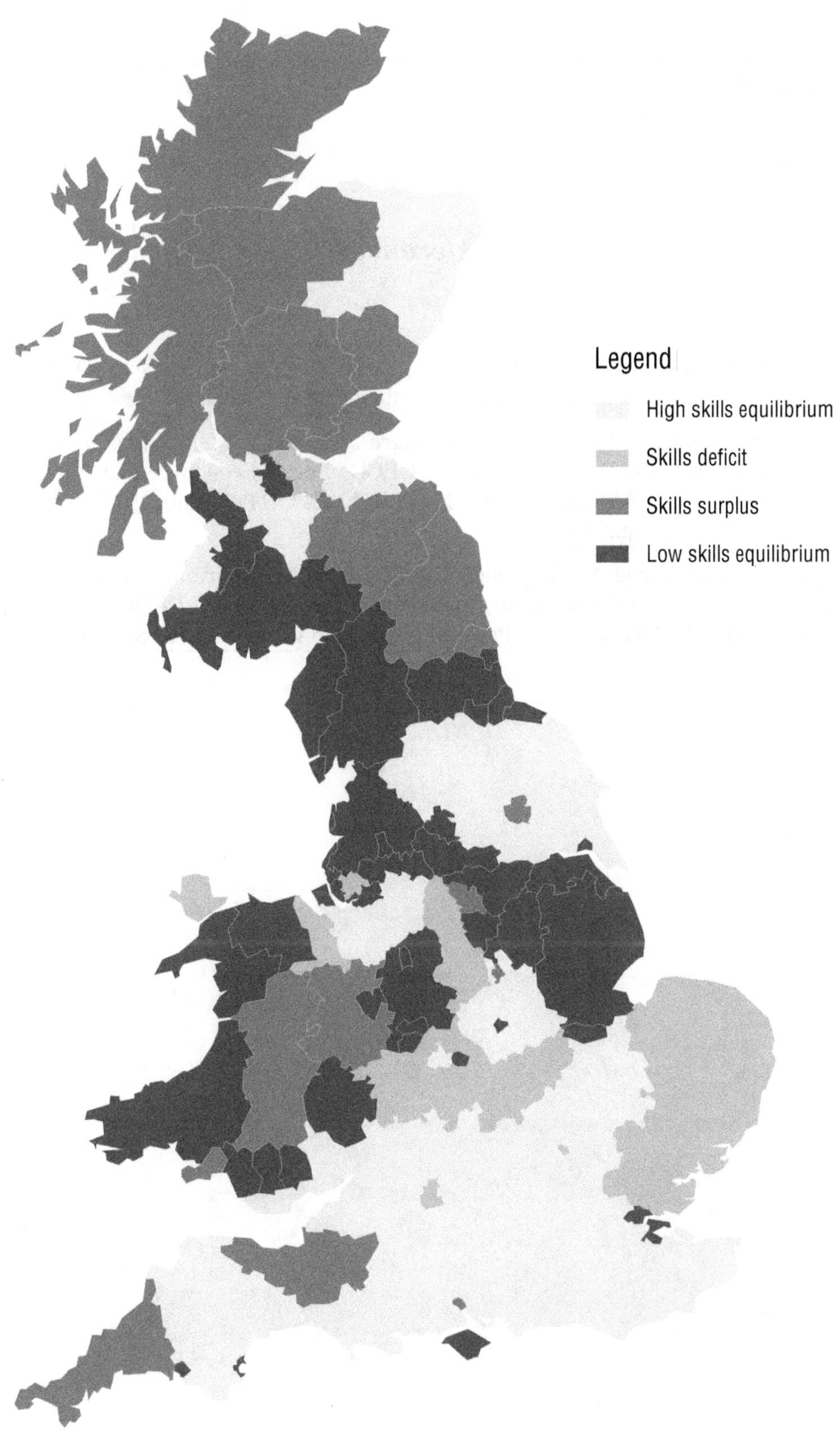

Note

1. The Derbyshire and Nottinghamshire LEP area has the same boundaries as the Derbyshire and Nottinghamshire NUTS 2 area.

References

Annual Population Survey (March-May 2014), Office for National Statistics (ONS), https://www.nomisweb.co.uk/query/select/getdatasetbytheme.asp?theme=28.

Froy, F. and S. Giguère (2010), *Putting in Place Jobs that Last: A Guide to Rebuilding Quality Employment at Local Level*, OECD Local Economic and Employment Development (LEED) Working Papers, No. 2010/13, OECD Publishing, Paris, http://dx.doi.org/10.1787/5km7jf7qtk9p-en.

Froy, F., S. Giguère and M. Meghnagi (2012), *Skills for Competitiveness: A Synthesis Report*, OECD Local Economic and Employment Development (LEED) Working Papers, No. 2012/09, OECD Publishing, Paris, http://dx.doi.org/10.1787/5k98xwskmvr6-en.

Chapter 3

Local Job Creation Dashboard findings in England

This chapter highlights findings from the local job creation dashboard in England. The findings are discussed through the four thematic areas of the OECD review: (1) *better aligning policies and programmes to local employment development;* (2) *adding value through skills;* (3) *targeting policy to local employment sectors and investing in quality jobs; and* (4) *being inclusive.*

Results from the dashboard

This section of the report presents the main findings from the in-depth fieldwork undertaken in England. In the following section, each of the four priority areas of the OECD review are presented and discussed. The full results of the Local Job Creation dashboard analysis for England are presented in Figure 3.1.

It is important to highlight that these dashboard scores represent a synthesis of responses from interviews conducted for this project based on a range of qualitative and quantitative information. They provide an indication of the relative position across the local case study areas in England on each of the themes and sub-criteria discussed. The full international results and dashboard comparisons can be found in *Job Creation and Local Economic Development, 2014* (OECD, 2014a).

Figure 3.1. **Overview of results from Local Job Creation Dashboard**

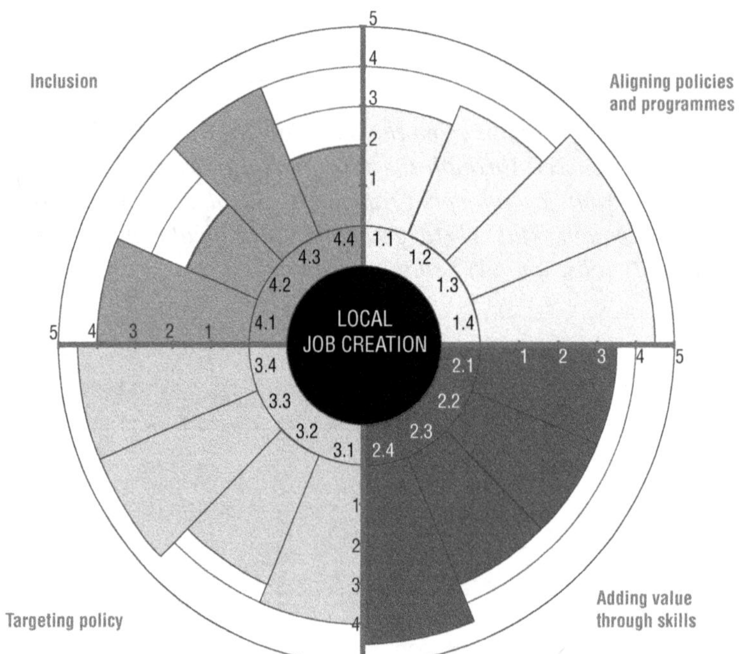

Theme 1: Better aligning policy and programmes to local economic development

Flexibility in the delivery of employment and vocational training policies

The OECD defines flexibility as "the possibility to adjust policy at its various design, implementation and delivery stages to make it better adapted to local contexts, actions carried out by other organisations, strategies being pursued, and challenges and opportunities faced" (Giguère and Froy, 2009). Flexibility deals with the latitude that exists in the management system of the employment system, rather than the flexibility in the labour market itself. The achievement of local flexibility does not necessarily mean that governments need to politically decentralise (Giguère and Froy, 2009). Governments just need to give sufficient latitude when allocating responsibilities in the fields of designing policies and programmes; managing budgets; setting performance targets; deciding on eligibility; and outsourcing services.

Figure 3.2. **Dashboard Results: Better aligning programmes and policies to local economic development**

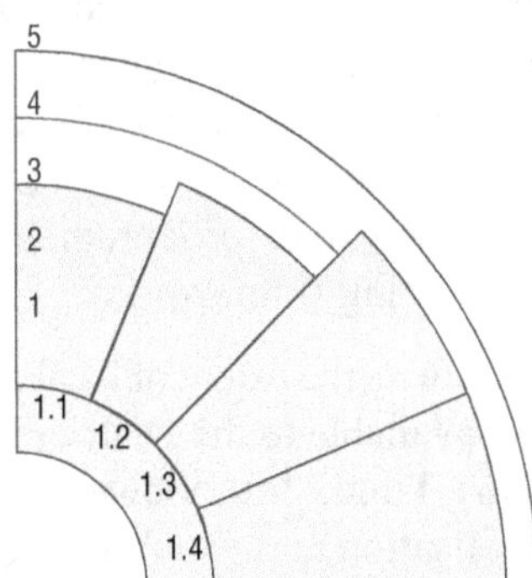

Flexibility and accountability of local Public Employment Service offices

Traditionally, the British Public Employment Service (PES) has been regarded as hierarchical with comparatively centralised delivery, and likewise the Department for Work and Pensions (DWP) has been viewed as one of the most centralised of any government department (Mosley et al., 2001). Over time, there has been a move towards greater decentralisation and local flexibility. However, eligibility criteria for types of support available are set at the national level and there is no local flexibility for eligibility to be varied. This was described by interviewees as being "frustrating" at times.

In 2002 Jobcentre Plus (JCP) was created with the merger of the Employment Service and the Benefits Agency, so combining together activation and benefit functions. At the outset, JCP performance management was via "Performance and Resource Agreement" targets agreed at the national level with DWP. At the forefront of these targets were "job entry" targets which were weighted through a points system which gave greater weight to placing in jobs those claimants, who on the basis of their characteristics, were less likely to gain employment. In 2006 a new Job Outcome Target (JOT) was introduced, which was designed to combine automatically information on people flowing off the benefits register with data on employment status from Her Majesty's Revenue and Customs (HMRC) (i.e. income tax records). However, because of the time lag involved in capturing data to measure this target, there was increasing reliance for internal performance management on an "Interventions Delivery Target" designed to ensure that service users undertook mandatory interviews and were referred to programmes at key stages of their benefit claim.

In 2011 a new "Performance Management Framework" was introduced which emphasises moving people off benefit into employment as quickly as possible. This is measured by benefit off-flows, measured at prescribed intervals of 13, 26, 39 and 52 weeks set by national government but the levels of which are set by JCP District Managers operating at the sub-regional level in accordance with local population profiles and economic conditions. Off-flow targets are designed to focus greater attention on employment outcomes – albeit off-flows need not necessarily be into employment. However, the National Audit Office has suggested that the focus solely on off-flows might result in advisers providing preferential treatment for clients likely to contribute to the achievement of short-term targets (NAO, 2013).

In terms of Jobcentre Plus support for job seekers claiming benefits, there is a "Jobcentre Offer", comprising a wide range of possible employment measures, with advisers being able to select flexibly between voluntary measures whilst having to impose time-specific mandatory referrals. Overall, however, the situation is one of national employment policies being delivered with limited flexibility in the application of resources to locally-defined priorities. The idea is that local managers and advisers have greater scope to target resources according to individual and local needs, rather than solely follow a nationally determined structure. There is a "Flexible Support Fund" which advisers can use to provide support directly to job seekers, including buying work-related clothes and equipment and provision of in-work travel costs. Local managers can use the fund for locally-specific "low value" procurement, although tenders have to be offered on the DWP's national contracting framework.

It is difficult to estimate the extent of local flexibility in terms of finance, but approximately 15% of the budget is available to the District Manager to apply at his/her discretion through the Flexible Support Fund. Interviewees emphasised the ongoing direction of travel towards greater localisation and flexibility, but noted that they are unable to alter the way in which major funding streams are used. Employment initiatives are also funded through the European Social Fund, the Big Lottery Fund[1] and other sources. This provides some degree of local flexibility, but often at the expense of stability and continuity of funding since much of the funding is short-term.

Part of the ongoing welfare reform programme in the UK has been the commissioning of large-scale prime contractors to deliver the Work Programme for long-term out-of-work benefit claimants. The Work Programme became operational in June 2011 and took quasi-market arrangements in the delivery of employment programmes to a new level in Great Britain. The 18 contract areas are at the regional rather than the local level. For example, there are two prime providers in the East Midlands (the region in which Nottingham and North Nottinghamshire are located) – A4E and Ingeus – operating from a variety of local offices working with a supply chain of sub-contractors. Some local organisations (e.g. City Works in Hull) deliver the Work Programme, but the extent of flexibility is restricted by the contracts under which they operate. A large proportion of funding from prime contractors is wholly dependent on sustainable job outcomes, with larger payments for those furthest from the labour market. There is limited prescription of minimum service levels in the "black box" delivery model (OECD, 2014b).

Over the period to 2016-17 the benefits system is being reformed as a Universal Credit (UC) is being introduced to replace six existing benefits (Income-based Jobseeker's Allowance, income-related Employment and Support Allowance, Income Support, Working Tax Credit, Child Tax Credit and Housing Benefit) with a single monthly payment. UC payments will reduce gradually as people earn more (e.g. benefit support will be gradually tapered away). Part of the rationale for UC is reducing the complexity of the benefits system and also ensuring that all benefit claimants who move into work are better off financially (i.e. the goal is helping people to be better off in work). There was little discussion of UC in the interviews and local roundtables since for most local partners it was not an immediate concern. However, it was recognised that it would mark a major change going forward.

Flexibility in local education and training provision

In England the "classic" route for students heading to higher education is to take a general set of GCSE (General Certificate of Secondary Education) qualifications at the age of 16 years, a smaller set of A (Advanced) level qualifications at the age of 18 years and then to proceed to university, to study academic or more vocational degrees. There are important ongoing reforms to education in England, resulting in a plurality of provision including: state schools,[2] academies,[3] free schools,[4] university technology colleges (UTCs),[5] studio schools[6] and private schools,[7] as well as FE Colleges.[8] The direction of travel is for the devolution of greater autonomy from Government to head teachers and college leaders to run their institutions and teach lessons as they deem appropriate, in the context of reforms to the national curriculum and reforms of the examination system.

Routes through vocational education at post-16 level are varied and complex. McCoshan and Hillage describe the English "VET system" as being "characterised by significant autonomy for colleges and other training providers on the one hand and voluntarism as regards employer involvement on the other" (McCoshan and Hillage, 2013). Post-secondary education is provided by a mix of further education and training providers (in the private sector but including not-for-profit and companies with charitable status). Private training providers often provide short duration provision for employed and unemployed adults, which can be flexible.

The Department of Business, Innovation and Skills (BIS) is responsible for policy and funding of adult skills development for people aged 19 years and over. Its regulatory and funding responsibilities[9] are discharged through the Skills Funding Agency (SFA). The Department for Education (DfE) is responsible for education up to the age of 18 years and its responsibility for funding is discharged through the Education Funding Agency (EFA). (The SFA and EFA replaced the Learning and Skills Council[10] in 2010.) BIS and the DfE work together on apprenticeships for 16-24 year olds. The National Apprenticeship Service (NAS) supports, funds and co-ordinates the delivery of Apprenticeships. Employment policy and training programmes for the unemployed are the responsibility of DWP.

As autonomous institutions incorporated by an Act of Parliament, in theory FE Colleges have the freedom to innovate and respond flexibly to the needs of individuals, employers and local communities. However, one interviewee said that in practice the "drivers are all national". While FE Colleges have been given increased "freedoms and flexibilities" over their budgets, it was noted by interviewees that it was not possible for transfers to be made between EFA and SFA budgets for Colleges. However, use of the Innovation Code (which allows colleges and training organisations to enrol learners on a course that at present does not lead to a Qualifications and Credit Framework (QCF) qualification) within SFA funding was mentioned by interviewees as a way of meeting local employer needs and addressing emerging skills deficiencies. Use of the Innovation Code is cited in the Nottingham City Deal as a mechanism to support plans for the delivery of provision and the development of new qualifications where gaps in the current education and training may exist.

The City Deal in the Humber sub-region (including Hull) will give the LEP some control over vocational training budgets. However, it is too early to say how this will work out in practice. LEPs are playing an increasing role in the use of European funding from the European Social Fund (ESF) for employment and skills. However, the LEPs need to make sure that activity does not duplicate or undermine national policy. ESF funding (including a Local Response Fund) can be used for activities such as increasing access for the most disadvantaged and supporting their retention and reducing drop-out, increasing participation whether there are current or predicted skills shortages and developing skills to meet future needs.

Government and other agencies in Hull and the Humber sub-region highlighted the extent of joint working on operational issues, especially around partnerships associated with the LEP. Jobcentre Plus and the SFA are key government agencies operating in the skills and employment fields. Informants acknowledged that the degree of joint working on strategic issues is limited by the perceived centralised nature of strategy and funding within the DWP (including the management of Work Programme contracts); however, day-to-day engagement by Jobcentre Plus on operational issues is strong. This observation was replicated in discussion with a number of agencies in Hull and Scarborough (e.g. fairly effective and positive local partnerships between different types of agency (including government bodies), but limited engagement of central government departments in joined-up strategic thinking at the local level.

While national and European funding streams are a key driver of activity, the VET system is relatively flexible. However, in England the institutional architecture[11] and policy environment has been (and are) relatively fluid and unstable. In a voluntarist system, this has hindered engagement of some local employers and can create confusion for some local stakeholders.

There is increasing recognition that universities and FE colleges are important anchor institutions in local economies. The Witty Review of Universities and Growth underscored the important role of universities in fostering growth at local and national levels, and recommended that alongside research and education, universities should make facilitating economic growth a core strategic goal (Witty Review of Universities and Growth, 2013). The engagement of universities and FE colleges in the local case study areas, especially on research of relevance to local sectors and their engagement with SMEs is indicative of such a role in facilitating local growth.

Capacities within employment and VET sectors

The PES and VET sectors have been negatively affected by reductions in public expenditure. One interviewee in Nottingham noted that freezes on PES recruitment "for a good while" had led to a lack of "new blood" and had implications for the demographic profile of the PES workforce, with a disproportionate number of staff in middle and older age groups. It was noted that this had provided a particular challenge in terms of the "digitalisation" agenda (e.g. keeping abreast of the way that more jobs are advertised online, necessitating an online response) and associated information and communications technologies (ICT) and social media. This meant that advisers needed to be able to advise claimants about suitable email addresses, loading CVs online and use of smartphones.

Similarly, in Hull austerity measures had led to a reduction in Jobcentre Plus staff. However, the indications were that staffing capacity remained sufficient to deliver the necessary services, given the range of local providers that can be called on to support.

In relation to VET, at the national level while the budget for schools has been protected in the face of government spending cuts, the budget for FE Colleges has not been protected. This has meant that FE Colleges have seen budget cuts for 18 year olds and for adults. However, in Hull the consensus of opinion among interviewees was that there is no real problem with capacity to deliver education and training, given that there are two large colleges, several private sector training providers and a number of providers of employment and related services in the voluntary and community sectors. In addition, Hull City Council has its own training arm. Scarborough is less well served than Hull in terms of further and higher education provision, and there are currently plans to develop a UTC in the area to address skill needs in the engineering sector.

In Nottingham there are two large colleges and private sector and community and voluntary sector training providers. In North Nottinghamshire, there is further education provision at a number of locations. Hull College is the largest FE provider in Hull. East Riding College has a centre in Hull and there are a number of smaller colleges in the city, for example Wyke College. Hull residents also attend Bishop Burton College, a specialist land-based college just outside the city. Yorkshire Coast College is the largest FE provider in Scarborough District; East Riding College has a centre in Bridlington and the University of Hull has a campus in Scarborough.

Policy co-ordination, policy integration and co-operation with other sectors

Collaboration within policy areas

Partnership working is generally strong in the case study areas. In the PES across Nottingham and North Nottinghamshire there is considerable emphasis on policy co-ordination and there are several examples of mechanisms to promote collaboration. Interviewees in Nottingham and North Nottinghamshire were generally extremely positive about the benefits of partnership working. One respondent said "local partnership work is the cement that holds it all together", citing how partners across different policy domains had come together in Local Strategic Partnerships (LSPs) under the previous UK Labour Government to work on Local Area Agreement (LAA) targets, and this local partnership working across policy domains had continued as "employment" and "tackling worklessness" issues had been placed on the policy agenda.

In relation to delivery of training by the not-for-profit/social enterprise sector there is some degree of voluntary co-ordination, albeit one interviewee described this as being quite "random". There is nothing in place from a statutory perspective to support such co-ordination. In Nottinghamshire, the Nottinghamshire Training Network is a membership-based organisation which represents local and national training providers and support organisations involved in delivering work-based learning, apprenticeships and employability provision. Colleges and schools are also members. It creates a collective "voice" for learning providers and promotes continuing professional development (CPD) across the learning sector. It works with key partners, such as the LEP, Nottingham and Nottinghamshire Futures (which manages the delivery of the National Careers Service in the East Midlands), local authorities, the National Apprenticeship Service and the Skills Funding Agency to increase economic growth and individual well-being across the area.

Similarly, in the East Midlands EMFEC (East Midlands Further Education Colleges) is a membership body providing umbrella services for colleges and providers in the further education sector. It is concerned with supporting members to operate effectively and collaboratively though support services including knowledge sharing, networking, professional development, conferences and facilitation of collaborative work. Historically, further education colleges have competed with one another, but there are increasing drivers to collaborate including, most recently, through LEP-related activity and bids for capital funding for the sector. Hence, colleges are increasingly working together. EMFEC has been, and is, heavily involved in the work of the Skills Commission in the D2N2 LEP area which brought together Employment and Skills Boards, representatives from the FE sector, universities, schools, the careers service, independent training providers and business representatives to formulate a Skills Strategy and Action Plan for the LEP.

Overall, however, in the words of one interviewee in Nottingham, further education colleges and the private training providers "co-operate and compete". Another considered that because of the multiplicity of small local training providers "the list [of providers] is endless" and that there was a great deal of competition creating a strategic need to "knit all the funding streams and providers together".

Similarly, discussions with stakeholders in Hull and Scarborough revealed many examples of organisations within policy domains working together to address commonly-identified issues. For example Hull and East Riding Colleges are working together – while recognising that they are competing in other fields – on the "Skills Support for the Workforce" (SSW) initiative designed to engage SMEs more fully in the training and development of their employees. Likewise, there are numerous examples that were cited of collaboration on skills and employment issues between organisations within the voluntary and community sector, for example those co-ordinated by the Humber Learning Consortium (HLC).[12] HLC was established in 2001 and has become an important local player, operating in the Humber sub-region and in other areas, notably South Yorkshire, albeit with Humber accounting for about two-thirds of their activities. HLC is a not-for-profit organisation and acts as a "management and quality hub", with around 40 partner organisations, mainly from the voluntary and community sectors, but also local authorities and independent providers. Training and employment initiatives are delivered through sub-contracting arrangements with partner organisations.

Collaboration between policy areas

Collaboration of local policy makers on employment and skills issues from PES, VET and economic development sectors is well-established and occurs on a regular and frequent basis; indeed, one interviewee felt that there were "too many" meetings.

Some interviewees in Nottingham and North Nottinghamshire felt that the nature of collaboration had changed over time. When EMDA (the Regional Development Agency for the East Midlands) was in existence, there was an emphasis on "joining up" across policy domains in the development of strategies. One interviewee felt that the amount of such "joint" activity had diminished with the establishment of LEPs, given their less clear remit, such that in practice, activity was driven by funding streams in which rules were set at the national level, with local policy makers having to bid for funds and deliver outputs and outcomes in accordance with national eligibility criteria which might differ from local strategic objectives. Nevertheless, as they are becoming more established, LEPs are becoming a clear focus for joint activity.

While the majority view is that the Humber sub-region was of working towards greater policy integration and co-operation in relation to employment and skills, some interviewees expressed the view that the system was not yet sufficiently well-integrated and that the LEP in particular was trying to do a challenging job with very limited resources. It was felt that activity had to rely heavily on the goodwill and commitment of partners, which in general is strong, but increasingly limited by capacity constraints in the context of continuing pressures on public sector funding. Local partners in Scarborough have been less well integrated to date in LEP activity,[13] perhaps reflecting the more limited involvement of District Councils than of upper tier local authorities with LEPs (a point also emphasised by district councils in North Nottinghamshire). Until recently, the York, North Yorkshire and East Riding LEP had given lower priority than many other LEPs to skills issues, a further factor influencing the relatively low level of engagement by Scarborough partners. However, this is likely to change with the implementation of the Strategic Economic Plan, which gives greater priority to employment and skills issues.

There are examples in Nottingham and Nottinghamshire of partnership working and co-location of services (see Box 3.1 for details of the Water Court Academy in Nottingham). In other examples, Nottingham City Council funds a number of community groups to undertake outreach work in local communities. There are also Job Shops at the community level providing skills training, interview preparation and advice. In Mansfield (in North Nottinghamshire), the Citizens Advice Bureau has created a multi-agency hub bringing together various services provided, including a Credit Union, and in nearby

Ashfield a multi-agency hub has been created in an old community hospital. A desire was reported to create similar multi-agency hubs elsewhere, to "achieve better cross-over and personalisation".

Box 3.1. **Water Court Academy, Nottingham**

As an example of co-location of services and local flexibility in PES provision, the Water Court Academy in Nottingham supports unemployed young people aged 16-24 years. It is a sector-based Academy, specialising in Hospitality, Retail, Care and Administration. Young people are referred to the academy in "warm handovers" from Jobcentre Plus offices in the city, and the idea is that "personal pathways" are developed for young people. Alongside personal advisers working with young claimants and business support staff, there are 19 providers (external to Jobcentre Plus) co-located within Water Court Academy. At various times, there are representatives from the Prince's Trust, the Territorial Army, Acromas Recruitment, the Careers Service, training providers and others. It is the site of an Apprenticeship Hub and a Nottingham Jobs Fund matching desk. The emphasis is on creating a welcoming environment, informed by regular customer insight exercises.

While the example of Water Court Academy relates to co-location of delivery, co-location can be important also at a strategic level. One factor that helps to facilitate collaboration between organisations working in different policy domains in Hull is the co-location of several organisations in one building: the World Trade Centre. This houses the Local Enterprise Partnership, UK Trade and Investment, Hull and east Yorkshire Bondholders and Team Humber Marine Alliance. In particular, this co-location brings together several organisations that are connected in different ways with the business community in the city and enables these groups to share intelligence and ideas, often in an informal way.

The Humber LEP has worked hard, with limited resources, to develop and build on the partnership working and relatively strong business networks that are characteristic of Hull and the Humber sub-region. For example the Employment and Skills Board has representation from across the spectrum of policy, educational and employer organisations and interviewees from these groups were unanimous in emphasising that this is a "real" partnership and not merely a "talking shop". The "Skills Pledge" – an initiative whereby employers are encouraged to contribute to skills and employability initiatives in schools and colleges – is a further example of partnership working across the city. A similar programme exists in Scarborough.

Collaboration with the private sector and area-based partnerships

Jobcentre Plus and VET stakeholders have frequent and ongoing connections with employers. The 2006 Leitch Review of Skills proposed the creation of a new integrated employment and skills service and also advocated the establishment of a network of employer-led Employment and Skills Boards (ESBs). This represented a step towards greater involvement of employers in strategic decisions about training and skills development initiatives to meet local needs.

In Greater Nottingham (and later Nottinghamshire) there has been a longstanding ESB; when it disbanded in March 2014 the Nottinghamshire City and County ESB was the longest running in England; (since then the local authority has been taking some of its activities forward). It was formed in 2004 and from 2010 extended its geographical reach over the whole of Nottinghamshire. It had a majority private sector membership and was independently chaired, but included public sector members (as major employers, drivers of economic growth and spenders in the local economy) and voluntary sectors members (playing a key role in delivery). A selection of its key roles and activities are summarised in Box 3.2.

Box 3.2. **Greater Nottingham/Nottinghamshire City and County ESB: Roles performed**

- Led the employment and skills regeneration partnership for Nottingham City Council's Local Strategic Partnership
- Was a learning partnership for the Learning and Skills Council
- Was the lead partner for the Nottingham City Strategy – a DWP-funded initiative fostering local partnership working to address spatial and sub-group concentrations of persistent worklessness; it was the first City Strategy Pathfinder nationally to co-commission services with DWP – so tailoring to services to local needs.
- As the lead accountable partner for the Nottinghamshire: Fit for Work Service (designed to provide support for people in the early stages of sickness absence from work) across Nottinghamshire.
- As the lead co-ordinator of the LEP City Skills Fund's Skills Plan and Labour Market Observatory
- As the developer of the Employer Ownership service – Employer First (funded under Employer Ownership of Skills Round 2).

The above activities included a range of regeneration funded and open and competitively funded programmes and projects. In total the ESB oversaw the commissioning and delivery of public and private sector funding worth approximately GBP 8.5 million.

Over the lifetime of the ESB, policies tended to stream funding, and hence strategy and delivery, down two separate channels: one with a business and employment focus (which included undertaking studies of sectors of particular importance to the local economy), and one with an economic inclusion focus – exemplified by local work as a pathfinder under the auspices of City Strategy which aimed to tackle localised concentrations of persistent worklessness and a pilot for the Fit for Work initiative which was designed to provide support for people in the early stages of sickness absence from work. Over time, there was recognition that these two channels were not mutually exclusive.

In the Humber sub-region, the strength of partnership working is exemplified by the Employment and Skills Board (ESB) initially having representatives from 14 local organisations and the Skills Forum which brings together around 100 providers. In addition to the main ESB and the broader Skills Forum, there are a number of other sub-groups which bring together relevant partners. While the existence of such structures does not necessarily ensure that partners work effectively together, the local case study research indicates that there is considerable commitment across the Humber region to ensure that the LEP's limited resources are enhanced by the active participation of local partners. At the time of writing the ESB brings together representatives of education/policy/public sector, Jobcentre Plus, East Riding College, Humber Learning Consortium, North Lindsey College, University of Hull, Skills Funding Agency, Hull College Group, Franklin College, Cristal, Clugston Group,

Andrew Jackson Solicitors, Press Association, Phillips 66, Chamber Training, Hull Esteem Consortium, Humber Chemical Focus/Catch and BOC Operations.

The LEP is in the process of recruiting additional members of the ESB, in an effort to expand and diversifying the membership, specifically in relation to employers, with a particular emphasis on increasing the representation of SMEs.

Joint working between local stakeholders and employers is an established feature of the local policy landscape. Despite a lack of mandatory social partnership arrangements in England (and the rest of the UK) collaborative and partnership working is encouraged by policy. All interviewees in Nottingham and North Nottinghamshire expressed the importance of links with employers and underlined that linking with employers and meeting employers' needs for training and skills development was the "direction of travel" in policy terms. This was echoed in Hull and Scarborough.

An example of local partnership working to serve local residents, meet the needs of the local labour market and to enhance work with employers – while avoiding the possible confusion posed for employers by a multiplicity of stakeholders, is the Employer Hub in Nottingham. Funded through the Nottingham City Deal, it is founded on partnership working between the local authority, Jobcentre Plus and other local agencies (see Box 3.3).

Box 3.3. **Employer Hub, Nottingham**

The mission of the Employer Hub is to create a co-ordinated, seamless, bespoke recruitment and training service that matches the supply and demand in the Nottingham labour market, with the *primary aim* of developing, delivering and sustaining a multi-agency approach that ensures local people can be connected to, and benefit from, local employment and apprenticeship opportunities. The Employer Hub aims to provide an integrated recruitment support package that is cost effective and coherent to employers, assisted via the appointment of a dedicated manager and co-ordinator for each employer using Employer Hub services. The benefits to employers are reduced administration costs, access to a wider pool of local labour with appropriate skills sets thought targeted promotion of opportunities (so meeting corporate social responsibility objectives by supporting local people into employment), access to bespoke pre-employment training packages, and advertisement of employment opportunities at no extra cost. Packages for employers can also include sifting, screening and matching of applicants against employer specifications, assistance with interview preparation and hosting of interviews, post-employment support for Employer Hub sourced employees, and assistance with premises via the Invest in Nottingham team.

Participation of employment and training institutions in local networks

As indicated above, Jobcentre Plus is active in local networks in all of the case study areas. It has been noted that Jobcentre Plus is guided to a large extent by national policies and procedure; yet Jobcentre Plus is actively engaged in several area and economic partnerships at a strategic level and also works with training providers to encourage them to flex their provision to meet local needs. For example in Hull, Jobcentre Plus used part of their Flexible Support Fund to support the "CatZero" project, which runs team building and related programmes for disadvantaged young people, inspired by the 2007-08 Round the World Clipper race.

It is clear that the direction of change for Jobcentre Plus is towards greater emphasis on collaborative working. Universal Credit (part of the welfare reform programme outlined above) will bring about new changes – and mean more onus on linking to other services. In February 2013, DWP and the Local Government Association published a Local Support Services Framework, setting out how advice and support services, covering policy domains such as health and social issues, and digital and financial exclusion, might be delivered through local partnerships including Jobcentre Plus, local authorities and community-based providers. This is set to further endorse and embed local partnership working.

Evidence based policy making

Evidence based policy which is continuously evaluated and accountable

All partner organisations consulted for the Hull case study provided examples of how their policies and programmes were informed by evidence, ranging from official statistics on employment and qualifications to specially-commissioned surveys and studies, market intelligence (especially in colleges), evaluation studies, learner feedback and informal intelligence derived from regular contact with employers. For example, Hull City Council has been working with consultants to bring together all of the available evidence to inform their Employment and Skills Strategy. They plan to commission further work to fill in the gaps and provide intelligence about future employment and skills trends. Scarborough Borough Council has commissioned a local skills and training needs survey of employers and has conducted training needs analyses in key sectors. Local partners were also engaged with employers to inform their policies and strategies. For example, the Careers Service at the University of Hull is in contact with around 2 000 employers in the local area, a major source of intelligence on employer requirement in relation to higher-level skills, while both Hull College and East Riding College have strategic advisory groups of employers that provide guidance on current and future skill needs.

Similarly, interviewees in Nottingham and North Nottinghamshire highlighted the importance of policies being informed by evidence and were also aware of monitoring of outputs and assessment of outcomes. As far as resources and time pressures allowed, they expressed interest in using local evidence – whether "hard" statistical information, "soft" intelligence or a combination of the two. Indeed, the D2N2 LEP has commissioned consultants to bring together information and analysis to inform its strategies.

Some interviewees in Nottingham expressed concerns that despite recognition of the importance of evidence-based policy making, in practice the situation was likely to be deteriorating – in terms of both the quantity and quality of the evidence base, and the capacity and resources of partners to use existing information and intelligence. One interviewee noted that EMDA had resources and had developed experience and expertise in compiling and analysing existing data to "tell a story", but with the abolition of the RDAs and cut-backs in the public sector (notably in research and intelligence functions in local authorities) some experience and expertise had been lost, while that which remained had become more fragmented. It was suggested that co-location of research and strategy across employment, skills, business support and other policy functions at EMDA (the Regional Development Agency in the East Midlands) helped ensure that information and intelligence was used in a "joined up" manner, such that its impact was maximised.

With fragmentation of expertise across organisations access to the relevant human capital to use research and intelligence was considered to have become more difficult, and with more pressure on resources there was less time and capacity to use information and intelligence. The universities in Nottingham are one of the key sources of research expertise, but this expertise is not freely available. Similarly, in Scarborough the local authority has worked closely with the Scarborough Campus of the University of Hull to research local economic trends. In summary, the key issues in intelligent use of information and intelligence to support evidence-based policy are strategic expertise, capability and capacity.

Organisational changes have made it difficult to "plug in" these in the current policy framework. In the D2N2 LEP area university expertise had been utilised to provide information and intelligence to inform strategy and policy, but this had been on a project by project basis. Yet utilising knowledge and expertise in the use of local data sources from local higher education institutions (on either a call off contract basis or by setting up local observatories), perhaps coupled with secondments of Government Statisticians – who could combine technical expertise and gain insights into the need for, and use of, data sources locally, could help in ensuring that strategies are founded and monitored on a robust basis.

Some concerns were also raised in interviews about sample size reductions in some spatially disaggregated national data sources, as sample sizes for surveys (notably regional boosts) were reduced. Nevertheless, interviewees made reference to research reports and to information and intelligence that informed strategies. In some instances a good deal of reliance was placed on data from national surveys with data disaggregated to the local level (e.g. the Employer Skills Survey funded by the UK Commission for Employment and Skills). Some users supplemented this information with other information from Sector Skills Councils and local intelligence.

Some organisations conducted their own surveys (e.g. the local Chamber of Commerce). However, the difficulty of getting reasonable rates and meaningful responses to business surveys and the pressures on businesses associated with responding to requests for information was highlighted. One interviewee considered that in terms of surveys of the training needs of employers it was difficult to get employers to articulate their needs because for a long period "we gave them a "supply led" programme rather than a "demand led" programme" (e.g. training providers indicated what was available rather than asking employers what they sought and then tailored provision to meet their needs). This past practice was considered to have contributed to difficulties in making a transition to the new demand-led orientation.

Ability to collect data and administer policies within travel to work areas

The key spatial units for current policy delivery are LEPs and local authorities. In the case of Nottingham and North Nottinghamshire the relevant LEP is D2N2, which encompasses the cities of Derby and Nottingham and the administrative counties of Nottinghamshire and Derbyshire. There is some fit between administrative boundaries and travel-to-work areas. Several interviewees highlighted strong commuting links between Derby and Nottingham (although each of the cities is the focus of a separate travel-to-work area (as officially defined on the basis of commuting flows recorded in the 2001 Census of Population).

The North Nottinghamshire area has a number of important subsidiary employment centres (notably in the Mansfield and Ashfield area) and has functional links with both Nottingham to the south and Sheffield to the north; (the northern-most district in Nottinghamshire – Bassetlaw – is in both the D2N2 LEP and the Sheffield City Region LEP); while this reflects functional ties, it also creates issues of accountability and "double counting" in terms of policy and evidence. In North Nottinghamshire there is a travel-to-work area focused on Mansfield and another focused on Worksop and Retford. It is possible to retrieve some official data for travel to work areas, but the main policy focus is on the LEP area and local authority areas. There is collaborative working within and across administrative boundaries.

All stakeholders interviewed within the Hull and Scarborough case study areas emphasised their commitment to developing policies and programmes on the basis of robust evidence. Informants mentioned a wide range of types of evidence, from informal feedback from employers to college courses or employability programmes, more formal, structured employer consultation (e.g. through the Humber Skills Commission) to analysis of publicly-available data (e.g. from the Office for National Statistics), use of skill survey data (e.g. from the UK Commission for Employment and Skills Employer Skills Survey), commissioning of bespoke local surveys of employers or communities, and economic analysis and forecasting for local economies.

While it is clear that partners in all case study areas are committed to evidence-based policy-making, a number of key issues were highlighted by interviewees during local roundtable discussions:

- First, as noted above, there is a broad conception of what constitutes legitimate evidence to support policy developments. For example, colleges consult key employers to gain feedback on the quality and relevance of specific programmes, but wider evidence (e.g. market research) is needed to inform the strategic development of the colleges' offer in relation to local economic needs.
- Secondly, as noted above, some concern was expressed about the extent to which robust data is available at a sufficiently disaggregated geographical level to enable local partners to make informed strategic decisions. Sources such as the Employer Skills Survey, for example, may provide broad indicators of skill needs at the city or sub-regional level, but it is difficult to discern sector or occupational trends. Likewise, falling sample sizes for ONS surveys such as the Labour Force Survey may constrain the extent to which partners can obtain reliable local statistics.
- Thirdly, concern was expressed about the extent to which the capability of local partners to analyse economic and labour market statistics has been eroded in recent years. In particular, the demise of the Regional Development Agencies has resulted, according to roundtable participants, in a reduction and dissipation of analytical capacity. Likewise, resource pressures on local authorities have reduced analytical capacity in those organisations. Having said this, local authorities remain active in economic and labour market analysis (see Box 3.4 for an overview of such activities in Hull and Scarborough).

Box 3.4. **Local authority economic and labour market analysis in Hull and Scarborough**

Hull City Council is developing an Employment and Skills Plan (ESP) that is intended to operate in the context of the wider Humber Skills Strategy being developed by the Local Enterprise Partnership. Hull City Council has contributed to the development of the Humber Skills Strategy and is active on the LEP Employment and Skills Board. Nonetheless the Council feels that it is necessary to develop a skills strategy for the city, for the benefit of the people and business of Hull. In order to inform the skills strategy, the City Council commissioned an economic development consultancy to undertake a review of the available evidence and to bring in together into a coherent evidence base to underpin the ESP. The Council recognises the importance of adopting a dynamic approach to understanding the economy and the future demand for skills; therefore they are in the process of commissioning a bespoke economic forecasting model for the city, as well as business surveys that use methodologies similar to the National Employer Skills Survey.

Box 3.4. **Local authority economic and labour market analysis in Hull and Scarborough** *(continued)*

Scarborough Borough Council has limited resources to undertake local economic and labour market research, but recognises the importance of understanding the supply of and demand for skills in the local area in order to inform local initiatives such as the Job Match programme. In 2008 Scarborough Borough Council commissioned a local Employer Skill Needs Survey. The Council's Employment and Skills Manager is undertaking research on skill needs in key local sectors, notably engineering and construction. With limited resources, Scarborough Borough Council is making use of external funding (such as the Coastal Communities Fund) and focusing internal resources on key sectors and issues (e.g. youth unemployment).

Theme 2: Adding value through skills

Figure 3.3. **Dashboard Results: Adding value through skills**

Sub-Criteria

2.1 Flexible training open to all in a broad range of sectors

2.2 Working with employers on training

2.3 Matching people to jobs and facilitating progression

2.4 Joined up approaches to skills

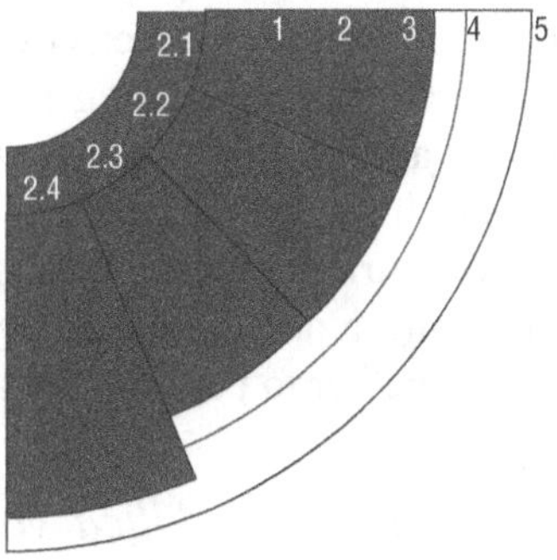

Flexible training open to all in a broad range of sectors

Training availability and funding

Most people in Nottingham have access to a wide range of training provision in a variety of sectors via two major further education colleges and private sector providers. Throughout Nottinghamshire, further education is delivered by several colleges from a variety of campuses. Residents in rural areas face most difficulty in accessing training, especially if they do not have cars, and in relation to public transport issues of both availability and cost were mentioned by interviewees.

From a training delivery perspective, given that funding is per learner model, there is an ongoing problem of training being uneconomic for small cohorts, especially in isolated areas. For some kinds of training, problems may be overcome through accessing training electronically, and this means that local residents/employers need not be tied to local suppliers. Access to training (in all local areas of England) is also shaped by affordability. The direction of travel in national policy is towards greater onus on employers and adult learners to fund their own training.

The extent of modular training varies by course. There were mixed views from interviewees in Nottingham and North Nottinghamshire regarding modular training, with some citing the danger of learners and/or employers "only picking the pieces they need" in the short-term, such that they may lack the "underpinning knowledge" that is essential for wider application and moving up to the next level. By contrast, others emphasised the importance of modular and/or bite-sized learning, especially for those who did not have a record of success in achieving formal qualifications when in compulsory education.

Interviews and analysis from Hull provided numerous examples of where employers – and SMEs in particular – felt that current training provision is not sufficiently flexible to meet employer needs. For example, funding usually requires that training leads to a full qualification whereas employers often need only modules (or no qualification at all). There is a tension here, at least in the short-term, between what might be in the best interests of individuals (who are likely to gain from the greater knowledge and more holistic context provided by a full qualification) and the employer (who might have a more specific immediate requirement). This suggests that there would be benefits from employers influencing the content of relevant modules (so that they are relevant to employer needs) to incorporate within existing mainstream frameworks, while individuals benefit from the portability of a full qualification in their future career.

In terms of sector/occupation, the impression is that there is an under-provision of training in relation to higher-level and intermediate engineering skills and managerial/ supervisory skills. This is a consequence of the city's history of low-skilled employment and is a key focus of current efforts to ensure that local people are able to take advantage of the opportunities offered by forthcoming investments in the offshore wind energy sector. Moreover, employers and providers observe that many candidates lack the necessary employability skills such as communication, time management and team working. Again, this is a central focus of current programmes to help people into employment. In Scarborough engineering, manufacturing and employability skills are felt to be under-supplied and local partners are working together to put together a bid to establish a UTC covering the district.

Unemployed people and lower-skilled workers and access to training

At the national level, there is a Skills Conditionality (SC) policy in operation. SC relates to claimants of Jobseekers Allowance and claimants in the Employment and Support Allowance (work-related activity group). These benefit claimants can be mandated to undertake training activity to address an identified skills need (e.g. in terms of literacy and numeracy support) which will aid their movement into work. The policy is designed to ensure that claimants are referred to relevant courses that will help them and that they start and finish such courses.

Further education colleges and training providers are expected to focus on the training offered to unemployed people on short, flexible courses tailored to the specific needs of unemployed people and local employers. One interviewee suggested that the emphasis of Jobcentre Plus on short courses for claimants was not necessarily in the best interests of unemployed benefits claimants, citing an example of a 16-week employer-led course at a college in Nottingham, while Jobcentre Plus wanted courses of 2 or 4 weeks in length. The D2N2 LEP has a policy of supporting Sector-Based Academies designed to support the needs of business, and includes pre-employment training relevant to the needs of a particular sector, a work experience placement and a guaranteed job interview.

It is important to note that eligibility for funding of training is determined at the national (i.e. England) level. There is full funding for training of adults aged 19 years and over in receipt of benefits for all learners up to a Level 2 qualification. For those adults on benefits aged 24 years and over, there are Advanced Learning Loans for those studying at Level 3 and above. Young people aged 19-24 years are eligible for full funding at the Foundation Learning level (i.e. pre Level 2) and for their first Level 2 and Level 3 qualifications.

Training in high level generic skills in VET curricula

There is an emphasis on generic as well as specific skills in accredited training programmes, in order to meet employers' needs and better equip individuals for employment. This is evident in the higher and further education sectors since "employability" is one of the indicators included in University "league tables". At the University of Hull, for example, the development of employability skills is high on the University's agenda, as part of an initiative to define the key characteristics of a "Hull graduate". While high level generic skills are recognised as important in their own right, their inclusion in a list of measures on which institutional performance is judged ensures that notice is taken of them, with local institutions often eager to emphasise what is specific about them.

Working with employers on training

Fit of training to employer demand

Interviewees in Nottingham and North Nottinghamshire highlighted that the emphasis on training provision was moving increasingly towards fitting with employer demand. Several interviewees highlighted that a challenge facing employers was changes in policies and programmes towards training.

As noted above, a shift from a "supply-led" training model towards a "demand-led" one requires employers to be able to express the outcomes they need from training. In an attempt to place the "employer voice" more centrally within decision-making about funding at the time of writing, the D2N2 LEP had set up Consultative Task Groups (with membership drawn from large and small employers, Sector Skills Councils, schools, colleges and independent training providers) for each priority sector – Transport Equipment Manufacturing (with a very strong focus in Derby and southern Derbyshire, but also a presence in Ashfield in North Nottinghamshire), Medicine and Bioscience (with a strong focus in Nottingham), Construction (across all areas), Food and Drink Manufacturing (one of the key foci is in North Nottinghamshire), the Visitor Economy (including attractions in Nottingham), and Low Carbon Goods and Services (all areas) – to conduct a skills gap analysis and a funding gap analysis to inform the development of a Skills Action Plan. The intention was to consolidate these Skills Action Plans to inform priorities for future expenditure of European funding on training.

More generally across all local case study areas, challenges in shaping further education college provision to meet employer needs include issues of timeliness (i.e. meeting business needs in a timely fashion), the fact that courses tend to be qualification led as opposed to meeting specific business need (which may not include qualifications) and that it is easier to deal with larger firms that can provide a greater volume of business. One interviewee highlighted that the two key performance indicators that the colleges are judged on by OFSTED (the Office for Standards in Education, Children's Services and Skills) are "success rates" and "timely completion", but went on to emphasise that these are not the priorities of employers. For instance, an example was cited by one interviewee of a major logistics firm being unable, because of business imperatives, to participate in training between November-January. The interviewee reported that if "timely completion [of a course leading to a qualification] fell in that window" the College would be disadvantaged in recording of outcomes of training. Another interviewee emphasised a lack of correlation between OFSTED gradings of Colleges and employers' behaviour in working with further education Colleges – hence underlining the point that what is valued by OFSTED and by employers may be different.

In Hull, the picture on working with employers on training is mixed. Many large employers and public sector organisations are active in working with colleges and other providers on training issues. For some employers (again typically the larger ones) this engagement extends to schools and colleges in a variety of other ways, such as placements, internships, project support and guest lectures. In Hull, there is also an Employability Pledge, where employers pledge to work with schools and colleges, and provide placements. In Scarborough, there is an Employability Charter to encourage employers to get involved with schools.

Further education colleges work on national initiatives designed to be responsive to local needs and priorities (as illustrated in Box 3.5). They also can and do demonstrate strong links with local businesses, led by the activities of Business Development/Engagement Managers. Examples of such links include Kia Motors and Central College Nottingham and the work of West Nottinghamshire College on Apprenticeship Frameworks with employers.

Box 3.5. **Examples of FE Colleges working with employers on training**

Skills Support for the Workforce (SSW) in the Humber sub-region

This project is funded by the European Social Fund and Regional Growth Fund, with the funding being directed through the LEP. It is a national initiative that is intended to be responsive to local needs and priorities, and the Humber programme is funded at GBP 3.5 million over two years, with a focus on upskilling people who are already in employment. SSW is being delivered in partnership with other VET providers across the Humber sub-region, including Grimsby Institute, North Lindsey College, Bishop Burton and East Riding colleges.

SSW is focused on SMEs and on LEP strategic sectors and skills identified by the LEP such as STEM, Renewables, Ports and Logistics, Chemicals, Health and Social Care, Creative and Digital-Tourism, Engineering, Construction, Manufacturing, Food and Agriculture. SME beneficiaries to date include a wholesale business that needed to train up its staff to support a shift from manual to mechanical handling and a renewable business that was supported to train five members of its administrative staff to enable increased business development activity in a growing sector.

Central College Nottingham working with Kia Motors UK

Central College Nottingham has worked in partnership with Kia Motors UK Ltd for over 4 years. The relationship started out with Kia renting space at the College's Automotive facility to deliver "technical training" to their Dealer Network. Since 2009, the relationship between the College and Kia Motors has developed and culminated in both parties agreeing to a long-term partnership to further the interests of both organisations. The commercial training facility saw the College and Kia Motors jointly invest GBP 250 000 to create a 17 500 square foot Kia Motors UK dedicated training centre which includes both technical and non-technical training facilities as well as a replica Kia showroom to cater for the training needs to the growing Kia Dealer network from across the UK. The national apprenticeship programme is designed to service the needs of the UK Kia dealer network with the ambition to have at least one apprentice in each Kia Dealership by 2015. Over the duration of the partnership, more than 700 apprentices will be trained in what is estimated to be worth over GBP 10 million to the local economy.

West Nottinghamshire College working with employers and sectors on development of Apprenticeship Frameworks

West Nottinghamshire College worked with employers in the corrugated paper industry facing the challenge of an ageing workforce to develop a flexible training programme incorporating the companies' in-house training programmes to improve business performance and engage new

Box 3.5. **Examples of FE Colleges working with employers on training** *(continued)*

employees. With the help of the Proskills Sector Skills Council, employers in the Fibreboard and Wood sectors were engaged. Work was undertaken with these employers to identify the key areas for performance improvements and raise their awareness of their skills gaps and improvements to performances that could be achieved. A new Apprenticeship framework was designed for the sector, incorporating the in house training programmes into a Technical Certificate which has been submitted for approval to the relevant awarding body. The employers who participated in the pilot were used as champions to promote the programme through their networks and the Sector Skills Council raised the profile of the new Apprenticeship. Agreement was reached on tools to be used to measure the improved business performance within the companies and measure distance travelled. The pilot apprenticeship programme have resulted in one local company, DS Smith, committing to this apprenticeship framework as part of their workforce development strategy plan until 2015 with an intake of between 10-15 new apprenticeships per year.

In Newark and Sherwood Council (North Nottinghamshire), the National Apprenticeship and West Nottinghamshire College worked together to tailor-make 100 apprenticeships at Clipper Logistics' Ollerton-based logistics academy on a site where employment is expanding. The opportunity to create the apprenticeships was borne out of the 100 Apprenticeship Campaign for Newark and Sherwood which was launched in January 2013, and was delivered in partnership by the Council and the National Apprenticeship Service (NAS). Existing members of staff undertake their NVQ Level 2 Warehousing Apprenticeships at the newly-created academy, to provide them with industry-recognised qualifications, together with additional support in literacy and numeracy where needed.

Extent of workplace training

Some information on workplace training is available from local sources, but such information is variable in quantity and quality. The type of information that may be available is illustrated by that collected on access to skills in the December 2012 Derbyshire and Nottinghamshire Chamber of Commerce business survey. This found that 85% of businesses surveyed had training budgets. On the job and induction training were the most common forms of training undertaken, followed by professional qualifications and National Vocational Qualifications (NVQs) between Levels 1 and 3. Nearly 30% of employers surveyed offered apprenticeships, sector specific or bespoke training to meet specific needs. The biggest barriers identified to provide training were time to release employees and cost. Almost 15% of businesses surveyed felt that there was either no provision to meet their specific needs or no provision locally.

Information on whether employers have business plans, training plans and budgets for training expenditure is also available at the local level from the UK Commission's Employer Skills Survey (ESS). The ESS is a representative sample survey across the England. The results showed that in 2013, 39% of establishments in Nottingham and 37% in Hull had a budget for training expenditure, compared with 27% in Nottinghamshire and 30% nationally. 70% of establishments reported that training had been funded or arranged for staff in the last 12 months, compared with 65% in Nottinghamshire, 72% in Hull and 66% across England. In all areas the main reason given by establishments for not training is that all staff are fully proficient: the relevant percentages were 60% in Nottingham, 70% in Hull, 71% in Nottinghamshire and 69% across England. In Nottingham the next most cited reasons for not undertaking training were no training available in the relevant area, the feeling that trained staff will be poached by other employers. In establishments providing training, 48% of establishments in Nottingham reported that there were staff that had been trained towards a nationally accredited qualification in the last 12 months; the respective figures for Nottinghamshire, Hull and England were 51%, 60% and 47%.

Apprenticeships

The promotion of apprenticeships is a key priority of the national government and local partners in England. Virtually all interviewees and attendees at local roundtables cited the importance of apprenticeships.

In Nottingham the City Deal has provided additional funding for apprenticeships, with the aim of providing apprenticeship opportunities supported by the Skills Funding Agency for Nottingham City residents aged 16-24 years and supporting local businesses to take on apprentices at intermediate (Level 2) or advanced (Level 3) level (see Box 3.6 for details).

Box 3.6. **Nottingham Apprenticeship Grant**

Any organisation within the Nottingham City boundary or within easy travelling distance thereof which employs less than 1 000 employees can qualify for the *Nottingham Apprenticeship Grant* which is worth between GBP 1 000-GBP 2 300 depending on circumstances. In an effort to promote sustainable jobs in order to qualify for the Apprenticeship Grant, there must be the potential for a sustainable job after the Apprenticeship has been achieved.

A grant of GBP 1 000 is available for a Level 2 Apprenticeship and of GBP 1 300 for a Level 3 apprenticeship, payable 13 weeks after the start of the Apprenticeship; before the grant is paid, confirmation is sought from the apprenticeship training provider that the young person is attending work and training regularly.

Employers based in the Creative Quarter (which is the flagship Nottingham City Deal project and the focus for Nottingham's Growth Plan, and which is home to incubators and clusters of technology-based companies in Nottingham's growth sectors of life sciences, digital content and clean technologies, as well as being a centre for independent retailers, bars and creative companies) can receive an additional GBP 500 and those who have been trading for less than two years receive an additional GBP 500. Hence a new business located in the Creative Quarter employing a Level 3 apprenticeship can draw down GBP 2 300 from the Nottingham Apprenticeship Grant.

The Nottingham Apprenticeship Grant is administered by Nottingham City Council's *Apprenticeship Hub*. By February 2014, there were 500 young people on the Nottingham Apprenticeship Grant.

In the Hull and Scarborough local case study areas, local stakeholders recognise the importance of enabling and providing high-quality apprenticeships in partnership with local employers. Humber LEP has established a team to promote and support apprenticeships, with one member focusing specifically on the "North Bank" (primarily Hull). Hull City Council is a major provider of apprenticeships in its own right, with around 100 apprenticeship places at any one time. Scarborough Borough Council is working with Groundwork, funded by the Coastal Communities Fund, to provide around 350 apprenticeship places in the district. Hull College currently has around 100 apprenticeship schemes, with around 2000 apprentices. The College feels that it is important to increase the status of apprenticeships and is actively trying to do so through promotional activities with both employers and potential learners.

City Works, a community/voluntary sector provider in Hull, is also active in supporting apprenticeships. They have worked closely with small and medium-sized construction companies to provide apprenticeship opportunities for young unemployed people. For example, City Works acts as host employer for the Esteem Consortium, which has been responsible for delivering several large-scale construction projects under the national "Building Schools for the Future" programme.

Training in SMEs

It is generally accepted that it is more difficult for SMEs than for larger employers to engage with training providers. This is a national issue that stakeholders need to address locally.

Drawing on evidence from sector skills agencies in the local area and wider region, the D2N2 LEP's *Skills for Growth Strategy 2013-2015* suggests that employers in SMEs may not be sufficiently organised to see the value of investment in training. This suggests a need to develop appropriate leadership and management skills so that they can plan effectively. Particular barriers faced by SMEs in pursuing training include the fact that off the shelf qualifications can be costly and inevitably cover areas not directly relevant to business needs, yet bespoke training is often expensive and difficult for a SME to commission alone and can be uneconomic for providers to deliver. Often SMEs are uncertain about whom to approach for training. Intelligence suggests that they have a strong preference for face-to-face support.

The Derbyshire and Nottinghamshire Chamber of Commerce and the Sector Skills Council for Science, Engineering and Manufacturing Technologies (SEMTA) have been active in working with employers to address some of these issues and source relevant training. For example, SEMTA piloted approaches where they grouped employers in Ashfield and Mansfield (towns in North Nottinghamshire) together to meet particular needs such as training Team Leaders, but also adding in additional relevant topics – such as lean manufacturing. The grouping of firms in this initiative creates economies of scale which can make training affordable, while also offering opportunities for continued networking and shared learning.

In Hull, concerns were expressed about getting SMEs to get engaged in training activities. The Skills Support for the Workforce (SSW) programme, described in Box 3.5 is beginning to address some of the issue facing SMEs in becoming involved with apprenticeships.

Matching people to jobs and facilitating progression

In England, there has been a National Careers Service (NCS) since April 2012. Prior to this, the Connexions Service provided guidance for young people and there were Education Business Partnerships promoting linkages between education and business.

The NCS is jointly managed by the Department for Business, Innovation and Skills and the Department for Education (with additional support from the Department for Work and Pensions and the Ministry of Justice). It offers an all-age service that is designed to meet the needs of adults and young people by delivering online, telephone and face-to-face services. The pressure is providing more information online at the national level so that it can be accessed by users at the local level including job profiles and sector-based information and through the telephone helpline with relatively little face to face support. To help support making information available that can inform people's decisions about their careers, the UK Commission for Employment and Skills is funding "LMI for All" to bring together existing sources of labour market information in an open data initiative that seeks to make relevant data freely available and encourage open use by applications and websites.[14] Face to face support is available to adults only.

Responsibility for young people's face-to-face services primarily resides with schools, colleges and local authorities; there is a statutory duty on schools to secure access to independent guidance for their pupils. From September 2012, schools have had a statutory duty to secure access to independent and impartial careers guidance for their students, and in September 2013, this requirement was extended to colleges. Research suggests that with the exception of a few schools which established innovative provision, in most schools this has resulted in deterioration in the level of careers guidance and that provision is both patchy and variable in quality (Andrews 2013). Indeed, a recent CIPD study has criticised the lack of support for young people during the transition from education to work, which is preceded by poor advice and guidance at school (CIPD, 2013). An initial report from the National Careers Council (2013) recommended that the National Careers Service should significantly expand its work with schools, young people and parents. Likewise a second report from the National Careers Council (2014) indicated that despite some signs of development, not enough action had been taken towards achieving genuinely relevant all-age careers service. Rather, it concluded that "the growing careers market is crowded, confused and complex with a multiplicity of disjointed careers provision" (National Careers Council, 2014: 4).

A report published by the official education inspectorate Ofsted on a study of careers guidance in 60 English secondary schools visited between December 2012 and March 2013 concluded that arrangements for careers guidance in schools were not working well enough (Ofsted, 2013). In particular Ofsted highlighted a relative lack of engagement of employers with schools-based careers guidance services. The report recommends greater attention to be paid to providing school students with work experience and that careers services should promote vocational training and apprenticeships more effectively with government playing a more proactive role in providing guidance and monitoring performance.

Illustrating what can be achieved through local partnership working, in Mansfield, North Nottinghamshire, the business community, the public sector and community groups come together with schools. In this area, the Mansfield Learning Partnership has been active in making links between schools, the public sector and employers and in providing work experience and careers guidance to young people, such that it has become "part of the fabric". Three local partnership organisations are centrally involved in the initiative:

- *Mansfield 2020*, created in 1991, is a local business-led partnership between the public and private sectors and community support organisations. Its primary objective is to promote innovation, support business investment and create a platform for dialogue between all organisations in the private and public sectors to promote innovation, support inward investment and create a platform for dialogue between all agencies in the private and public sectors to help build a strong business community and boost the local economy.
- *Mansfield Area Strategic Partnership* is facilitated by Mansfield District Council which provides a co-ordination function between public services that operate in Mansfield and the business and local communities.
- *Mansfield Learning Partnership (MLP)* is a soft confederation of six secondary schools in Mansfield, with a Director and support staff who reports termly to an executive group comprised on head teachers, wholly funded by them, liaises between schools and businesses.

Details of the programmes and activities that have been developed by the partnerships, in consultation with young people, are outlined in Box 3.7 – see Hutchinson and Dickinson (2014) for further details.

Box 3.7. **Mansfield Learning Partnership – frameworks and programmes**

Through a co-creation model for career related learning the following frameworks and programmes have been endorsed by the Mansfield 2020 Board and head teachers:

- A *partnership careers and employability framework*: a collaborative programme of career and work related education activities for Key Stage 3 and post 16 learners, which embeds: *(1)* self-development through careers and work-related education; *(2)* finding out about careers and the world of work; and *(3)* developing skills for career well-being and employability.
- A *partnership work experience policy*: sets a clear aspiration for offering a broad range of work experience opportunities including work placements, volunteering, work shadowing, internships and part-time and casual work. The MLP are working with local employers to provide work placement programmes for young people with meaningful and inspiring experiences whilst demonstrating to the local business community that they build their talent pipeline through quality work placements.
- A *local career related learning programme*: other opportunities to learn about careers and the world of work include:

a. *Junior enterprise event*: This event targets year 9s (13-14 year olds) and has a "MadebyMe theme". Enterprise activities offer opportunities to learn and develop the entrepreneurial characteristics of tenacity, independence, innovation, imagination, risk taking, creativity, intuition and leadership. The aim of this challenge is for participants to develop an understanding of how to set up a small business enterprise to sell a product, including the costs and responsibilities involved.

b. *Short story competition.* A local employer who felt very strongly about improving young people's literacy skills, confidence and self-belief sponsored a short story competition open to students aged 11 – 19. Entrants and winners attended an event hosted by a national radio DJ where they were asked to reflect on the skills they have demonstrated and their importance to the workplace alongside a celebration of achievement. Evidence of their achievement will be a publication of the winning stories printed by another local company.

c. *Post 16 master classes.* These bring enthusiastic, knowledgeable and authoritative local speakers who are leaders in their field into schools. The speakers address a group of students and describe their educational and career journey and talk about the challenges they have faced and what they consider their achievements to be. They aim to motivate and inspire young people and answer their questions.

d. *Sponsor a Student Programme*: This enables students in 6th Forms (i.e. those aged 17/18 years) to attend the Mansfield 2020 breakfast events and meet local employers. This experience helps students develop networking skills and the confidence to make decisions about their future career. Students apply to attend the networking meetings and then participate in a short workshop session beforehand to help them understand what to expect and to learn how to network effectively. MLP tries to place each student with an employer that the student has a career interest in the business. This is both popular and has seen some successes with some young people having secured work experience and employment.

e. *Business mentors.* Local employers act as Business Mentors to support employability related programmes which are funded by Mansfield District Council. Working with small groups of around 6-8 young people a local business person will run sessions on SWOT analysis, CV's, covering letters, interview roles plays, assessment centres and giving Top Ten Tips for success.

At the college and university level, careers services are active in linking graduates to local and national opportunities for careers events and jobs fairs. At the university level, this has become increasingly important given the profile of the "employability agenda". The Careers Service at the University of Hull, for instance, has been active in making links with local SMEs and seeking opportunities for graduate employment, internships and placements to raise awareness among employers about the benefits of employing highly-qualified people and equally to promote the SME sector as an attractive employment destination for the University's graduates. The Careers Service has identified a number of barriers to local graduate employment including low starting salaries (relative to regional centres such as Leeds, for example) and limited understanding among many employers about what they might expect from a graduate. Employers expect graduates to have the precise skills that they are looking for (e.g. specific engineering skills) and may not appreciate the wider benefits of employing a highly-qualified person. For SMEs in particular, there is often an issue of timing, with most graduates coming onto the market during the summer months, whereas employers tend to need people at specific times to meet specific needs.

To date, there has been little policy focus on helping low qualified people progress in work; the main emphasis has been on getting people into work. In large measure, this is a consequence of where public funding has been targeted. With increasing recognition of issues of in-work poverty – which in the UK outstrips out-of-work poverty amongst the working age group – and skills utilisation there may be more emphasis on work progression in the future, but to date this has largely been an issue that has been left to businesses, albeit promoted in some settings by trades unions though Union Learning Representatives (ULRs). Given the continuing growth of the UK economy, and with it the likely emergence of skill shortages, there is an important window of opportunity in the short- and medium-term for greater traction on in-work progression.

Activation and job matching services

Activation policies are designed at the national level and policies are implemented locally in accordance with national regulations. One of the key aims of Jobcentre Plus is to provide effective advice and support for benefit claimants looking for work. Hence, Jobcentre Plus is the organisation that is most directly concerned with matching unemployed people with the available jobs and it has explicit targets to place as many people as possible into jobs at different stages of unemployment (measured in weeks).

The first face-to-face contact job-seeking claimants have with Jobcentre Plus is a "new claimant interview" with an adviser. The purpose of this interview is to outline what is expected of the claimant in return for benefit (i.e. to set out the conditionality regime) and also to build up a picture of each claimant's employment support needs and identify barriers which might prevent them from returning quickly to work. Typically, this interview will capture information on claimants' personal characteristics (i.e. gender, age, lone parent status), benefit claim history, and income and capital. In this and subsequent regular interviews, challenges faced in accessing employment – including skills needs, health related support, childcare and/ or adult caring responsibilities – are assessed. Note that advice and support provided is not regarded as "counselling"; rather individual benefit claimants requiring specialist support or counselling may be referred to other partners locally able to provide such expertise.

A recent report by the House of Commons Work and Pensions Committee underscored the importance of a thorough and systematic face-to-face assessment of claimants' potential barriers to employment at an early stage of unemployment benefit claims, but also noted that some witnesses providing evidence to the Committee were concerned that the balance of the employment support process was overly focused on compliance monitoring, as opposed to meaningful and in-depth employment advice and support (House of Commons Work and Pensions Committee, 2014). Some interviewees also expressed concern about the balance between compliance monitoring and employment support activities.

At the initial interview, as of April 2014, and in advance of the national introduction of Universal Credit, the Claimant Commitment (designed as part of Universal Credit) has been rolled out across all Jobcentres. The Claimant Commitment sets out clearly and specifically what claimants must do to find work in return for support from state benefits; and this may be accessing specific support to overcome barriers to employment (such as specialist counselling and drug treatment). In general, the onus is on ongoing, full-time job search activity. However, the Claimant Commitment is also associated with enhanced flexibility for tailoring Work Plans to individual claimants. The name "Personal Adviser" (which was introduced under the UK Labour Government's New Deal programmes in the 1990s which were based on personalised delivery) has been replaced with a "Work Coach". As one interviewee noted, this demonstrates the focus on employment and also emphasises the expertise of the Work Coach on issues relating to recruitment processes and access to employment.

Claimants who have been on the Work Programme for two years return to the Jobcentre Plus "offer". Work Programme returners are a challenging group to place in employment. The performance of the Work Programme nationally has been below expectations except for young people; but statistics are not available at the local level. From April 2014, Jobseekers Allowance claimants come under the auspices of the Help to Work programme and are expected to be on a training scheme (for example, for literacy and numeracy support), a community work placement or take part in intensive work preparation and job search, losing their benefit if they fail to comply).

Alongside and in addition to the "official" programmes, there are other initiatives to help people into work. For example, in the Hull area, Construction Works has worked closely with some developers to help local residents to obtain jobs in the construction industry. A linked programme, run by sister organisation City Works, placed unemployed people in jobs created as a result of the opening of a large shopping centre in Hull. In Scarborough, in recognition of the problems faced by many young people, and informed by research, Scarborough Borough Council established Scarborough Job Match, delivered by Groundwork and a recruitment agency. This has been successful mainly due to the fact that it works with both employers and young people to identify and deliver the employability skills that are required. Further details of these activities are presented in Box 3.8.

Box 3.8. **Local initiatives and interventions helping residents into work in Hull and Scarborough**

Construction Works and City Works, Hull

In Hull, Construction Works (and its partner organisation City Works) have for many years been working with employers in the construction industry to help them to employ and train local people, often from disadvantaged groups. CW was established as a not-for-profit organisation in the early 2000s by the then regional development agency, Yorkshire Forward, and a local regeneration company, One Hull. Their initial focus was on helping small companies with bid writing, but soon became involved with employment-related activities, including work with Jobcentre Plus. This led CW to work with several major developments, including "The Deep" sea life centre and St Stephens Shopping Centre. At the time of writing CW has close links

Box 3.8. **Local initiatives and interventions helping residents into work in Hull and Scarborough** *(continued)*

with construction company Keepmoat and Hull City Council, working to engage local people in construction projects. For example CW helped around 1200 local people into jobs, including those who found work in the retail outlets as well as those engaged in construction activity. One interesting consequence of this initiative was that CW found itself helping to "back-fill" vacancies that were created in local retailers as a consequence of their employees finding jobs in the chain stores in the shopping centre, thereby creating a "trickle down" effect. City Works operates as a group incorporating a number of initiatives including Construction Works.

Scarborough Job Match

Scarborough Job Match (SJM) is an initiative established by the Scarborough Borough Council, with financial support from the Coastal Communities Fund. Scarborough has a number of areas of deprivation and the Scarborough Employer Needs Survey identified issues of limited employability skills among some of the district's school leavers. Job Match was established to address these issues. A key feature of the project is that it works with both young people and companies. Between 2010 and 2013, SJM worked with over 3 000 unemployed people and placed 1 000 into jobs with around 300 companies.

Joined up approaches to skills

Attraction and retention of talent

Nottingham has two universities – Nottingham University (which is a member of the elite Russell Group of research-intensive universities in the UK) and Nottingham Trent University (a leading former Polytechnic which traditionally has had a more local orientation) – and as such is a net importer of higher education students (particularly in the case of Nottingham University). It is an exporter of students on graduation.

Several interviewees felt that it would be in Nottingham's interests to retain more graduates, so enhancing the city's knowledge intensity. Indeed, one of the elements in "Realising the Nottingham Vision" set out in the Nottingham City Deal is to "attract and retain graduates to fill the new high-skilled jobs and drive economic development". However, another perspective was that young highly qualified people are the most mobile section of the population and so it may be futile to have a policy with the specific aim of retaining graduates. Rather, an appropriate policy would be on of raising the demand for high level skills; in the long-term, this might result in greater retention of graduates.

There is no university based in North Nottinghamshire but some further education Colleges have some higher education provision. There is a relatively low percentage of graduates in the area. In an attempt to retain graduates in the area by giving them an insight into the types of jobs available locally, in Mansfield and Ashfield, the local council has supported use of the European Regional Development Fund (ERDF) to highlight opportunities for graduates in the local area. The two initiatives in Box 3.10 exemplify how a local council, employers and schools can work together for the benefit of students/ graduates and the local economy.

The Careers Service at the University of Hull noted that historically, local employment and skills strategies tended to focus on lower-level blue collar skills, with limited interest expressed in higher-level skills, including those of graduates from the University. One

Box 3.10. **Local initiatives to retain graduates in North Nottinghamshire**

AimHigher is a locally-funded initiative designed to place undergraduates from the local area with businesses in order to gain work experience on a specific tangible project (e.g. in e-commerce, marketing, design, and energy efficiency) lasting 8 weeks during the University summer vacation. The undergraduates are paid a weekly training allowance of GBP 267. The scheme contributes 80% of this cost to SMEs, with the remainder being paid by the business. The businesses benefit from the project placement and commit to helping the student to benefit from developing their skills in a business environment. For the undergraduates participation in *AimHigher* working on a particular project is a positive feature for a CV. The undergraduates are engaged with via schools (i.e. before they go to University).

Graduates into Enterprise provides for fixed-term placements (maximum 6 months) of recent graduates or postgraduates with local firms, with the graduate working on a structured business project relating to the (post)graduate's skills and experience. By the end of the placement the business should have been able to identify a tangible improvement in business performance. Ashfield and Mansfield District Councils contribute 50% of a weekly training allowance of GBP 267 to SMEs. The Graduates into Enterprise Team discuss project requirements and endeavour to identify and recruit graduates. It is this "matching" that is crucial to the success of the initiative. The same team monitors the progress of the graduate and benefits to the company. Due to the resources involved in these activities, the scheme is difficult to scale up. However, for businesses, the scheme aims to help businesses' growth and expansion plans, improve operating efficiency and competitiveness, and increase profitability and competitiveness. For graduates, the scheme is designed to help develop skills in a business environment and potentially benefit from a permanent employment opportunity. Local economic benefits can include retention of highly skilled individuals.

consequence of this has been that, despite the fact that 50-60% of University of Hull students originate from the Yorkshire and Humber region, it appears that significant numbers of graduates go on to jobs in large urban centres such as London, Leeds, Manchester or Sheffield, with relatively few finding graduate jobs in the Humber sub-region. Localised graduate pay differentials are attracting many graduates to work in cities such as Leeds (about 100 kilometres from Hull), where starting salaries tend to be higher than in Hull and Humber. Limited data means that it is difficult to assign precise numbers to this trend, but qualitative evidence from students, graduates and employers appears to back up these observations.

The University of Hull is looking closely at the potential for small businesses in the local area to generate demand for graduates. One of the perceived barriers to SMEs employing graduates is salary (the average Hull graduate salary last year was approximately GBP 20 000). The Federation of Small Business (FSB) has stated that 90% of small firms will never employ a graduate.

The University of Hull Careers Service is active in networking with employers. The Careers Service has 4000 employers on their database, of which about 2000 are in the local area. The experience of the Careers Service is that most employers have a positive view of the university; however some employers express concern that the skills developed by university graduates do not always meet their requirements.

The University of Hull recognises that there is a need to attract a larger high-tech high-skills knowledge base to Hull, especially in the light of new investments in offshore wind energy and associated sectors. The University is undertaking an extensive curriculum reform process, one element of which is to ensure development of relevant employability skills in the context of research-led degree programmes.

The graduate internship programme currently being operated by the Careers Service and funded by the Higher Education Funding Council for England (HEFCE) is providing paid internships for graduates for up to 12 weeks. The University is able to offer employers a subsidy to take on graduate interns. Careers Service respondents felt that the internship programme is a positive experience for both graduates and employers, which also helps to build links with other University activities including research and knowledge exchange The programme includes large businesses (for example Smith and Nephew and Reckitts) but there is a push to attract more small businesses onto the programme.

While it is clear that there is more to be done to retain talented graduates in the region and to encourage local business to make use of the high-level skills available in the area, the University of Hull Careers Service noted that some local small employers are significant employers of Hull graduates, including growing businesses such as Summit Media, Jesmond Engineering and Garthwest.

Joined up local skills strategies

Partners in all local areas stated that they were working towards a joined up approach to skills and highlighted the importance of partnership working. The work of the LEPs indicates that this is moving from being an aspiration towards becoming a reality. At the time when case study work was undertaken, the LEPs were developing the Strategic Economic Plan and associated skills strategies. In July 2014, local growth deals were announced (see Box 3.10 for a summary of The Humber Growth Deal).

Box 3.10. **The Humber Growth Deal – Selected Summary**

The Humber Growth Deal is designed to support the economic ambition of the Humber Local Enterprise Partnership (LEP) to "maximise the potential of the Humber Estuary and to become a renowned national and international centre for renewable energy… It will also help develop strengths in other key growth sectors, support businesses to grow, and help the residents of the Humber to access the opportunities they need to lead prosperous and rewarding lives."

The Growth Deal is intended to bring together local, national and private funding as well as "new freedoms and flexibilities" to focus on four key priority areas as identified in the LEP's Strategic Economic Plan:

- Creating the infrastructure that supports growth, including transport and housing;
- Supporting businesses to succeed;
- Creating a skilled and productive workforce;
- Stimulating economic development through further investment in flood and coastal risk management.

The Humber LEP has secured GBP 103.7 million from the UK Government's Local Growth Fund. Together with an anticipated GBP 240 million of local investment, this will create additional investment of over GBP 340 million between 2014 and 2021, with an anticipated 7 000 additional new jobs to be created across the sub-region.

Box 3.10. **The Humber Growth Deal – Selected Summary** *(continued)*

In relation to employment and skills, the Growth Deal is intended to support the following initiatives that are linked to the wider Strategic Economic Plan:

- A GBP 7 million new training infrastructure to provide a range of specialist offshore wind provision, including new facilities for working at height and marine transfer/ offshore survival training;
- Extension of Goole College's vocational skills workshop and associated classroom refurbishment to provide engineering and renewable technologies training
- Creation of a GBP 7.8 million new build logistics learning centre by Grimsby Institute providing renewable, STEM and environmental technology skills

The Growth Deal document concludes that: "Improving skills levels is a key factor in stimulating local growth and taking advantage of new economic opportunities. The LEP and the Government are committed to ensuring that adult skills provision is increasingly responsive to the needs of business and supports local economic growth and jobs."

The D2N2 Growth Deal is intended to build on the area's clear strengths by investing in a number of major projects in the LEP's priority sectors – including advanced transport engineering (which is especially important in Derby) and life sciences (concentrated in Nottingham). It brings together local, national and private funding, as well as "new freedoms and flexibilities" focused on skills and employability and rural business growth, based around 3 priority areas: *(1)* Enabling innovation-led growth; *(2)* Enhanced transport, employment and housing; and *(3)* A D2N2 Skills Deal.

The D2N2 LEP has secured GBP 174.3 million from the UK Government's Local Growth Fund. Together with an anticipated GBP 380 million, this will create a total new investment package of GBP 554.3 million for the LEP area of local investment, which is intended to deliver (in the employment and skills domain) at least 18 000 jobs and support over 147 000 learners by 2021.

Specifically in relation to employment and skills, the Growth Deal is intended to support the following initiatives that are linked to the wider Strategic Economic Plan:

- An expansion of floorspace next to Biocity in Nottingham to accommodate growing firms and allow space for new start-ups;
- The Nottingham Skills Hub project to integrate FE provision and employment opportunities across the city to meet the demands of business with a new College building in Nottingham's Creative Quarter, with employment sites in communities, which will complement the existing Work Programme, Youth Contract, Employer and Apprenticeship Hubs
- The Vision University Centre, Mansfield which will create a new teaching and learning space with state of the art facilities to support local people gain higher level vocational skills. Creating opportunities to access higher level skills locally will support increased progression among young people and is intended to ensure employers can access the higher level skills they need

- A new Chesterfield Centre for Higher Level Skills intended to deliver a huge change in higher level skills opportunities and support the economic growth of businesses and the workforce in Chesterfield and North East Derbyshire

The Government expects D2N2 LEP to open up new jobs associated with the Local Growth Fund to local unemployed and long-term unemployed people working closely with local and national back to work initiatives. This is part of a wider expectation that local areas use the Social Value Act, drawing on best practice across local councils and central expertise in maximising social value.

Theme 3: Targeting policy to local employment sectors and investing in quality jobs

Figure 3.4. **Dashboard Results: Targeting policy to local employment sectors and investing in quality jobs**

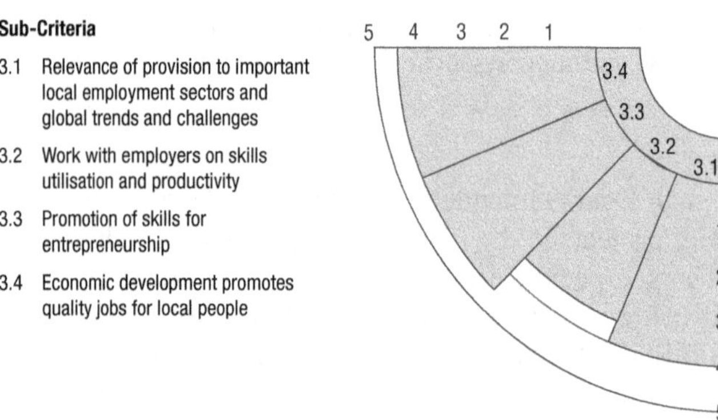

Relevance of provision to important local employment sectors and global trends and challenges

Relevance of provision to local employment sectors

A central tenet of the work of LEPs is to identify those sectors that are likely to grow in the future and ensure that their skills needs can be met. For example, in Hull, important sectors in the city currently are logistics and chemicals, but the major focus of skills planning is on the emerging offshore energy sector, with 1 300 jobs to be created directly by Siemens and other investment, plus associated supply chain opportunities. Scarborough will also benefit from the offshore wind investments through supply and repair operations. In Scarborough, potash mining is also planned to increase in the area and there will be skills and employment implications from this, while engineering and tourism are still important sectors for the local economy. A significant amount of work has gone into planning for the skills needs of emerging sectors and also ensuring that currently important sectors have an adequate skills supply. In addition, in Hull policy makers and providers are looking at the potential employment and skills implications of the designation of Hull as UK City of Culture in 2017.

The D2N2 LEP (which includes the Nottingham and North Nottinghamshire areas) has undertaken and is continuing to undertake work to support priority sectors such as Transport Equipment Manufacturing, Medicine and Bioscience, Construction, Food and Drink Manufacturing, the Visitor Economy, and Low Carbon Goods and Services. In early

2014, a skills and funding gap analysis was undertaken to inform the development of a Skills Action Plan for each of these priority sectors. The LEP is promoting the development of a Sector Growth Agreement Plan for each sector. Other "core employment sectors" (which are important in terms of the volume of employment opportunities [especially at entry level] and churn and "replacement demand") have been identified – including Health and social care, Retail and Logistics. Examples of the types of skills and training issues identified for selected sectors are outlined in Box 3.11.

Box 3.11. **Skills and training issues in key sectors in the D2N2 LEP area**

- *Life sciences* – there is a high percentage of graduates and postgraduates in this sector; there is a need to develop technician training and develop more opportunities for advanced apprenticeships; business management skills is an issue in developing new firms.
- *Low carbon* – strong demand for qualifications at Level 4 or above; requirement for scientists, technicians and engineers with training or transferable knowledge; skills to design and adopt technologies, products and processes to minimise carbon emissions.
- *Food and drink* – the focus tends to be on training to meet the regulatory environment, but business skills and developing and promoting career pathways are priorities.
- *Visitor economy* – characterised by a young workforce and high labour turnover, with a relatively high proportion of part-time working; good customer services skills and flexible attitudes are required; there is a range of entry level jobs but opportunities for progression need to be promoted more; management and leadership skills are needed to develop opportunities; there are shortages in chefs and managerial roles.
- *Logistics* – wide range of roles and skills levels; experienced drivers in demand but an ageing element of the workforce; demand for numeracy skills and competency with IT systems in supply chain management.

Relevance of provision to changing employment associated with global trends

One example of a partnership approach which is attempting to align skills development and training provision in a specific local priority sector in Nottingham and Nottinghamshire with global growth prospects is Employer First (see Box 3.12). The low carbon sector has been identified as critical to the transition to a green economy, and as such the work of Employer First is of relevance to the offshore energy sector in the Humber (sub-region).

Box 3.12. **Employer First**

Employer First is a not for profit employer-owned co-operative organisation. It is led by a Nottingham-based precision engineering company: FilterTechnic. Employer First aims to use investment from employers and from *Employer Ownership of Skills Pilot* funding to develop end-to-end skills and employment solutions, backed by industry. The service is being developed in response to the needs of the Low Carbon sector and marks a move away from a supply-led approach to skills by placing ownership and control of skills and training provision in the hands of employers.

Box 3.12. **Employer First** *(continued)*

Key objectives are to stimulate:

- Employer investment in apprenticeship training and workforce development
- Design of a "skills engine" to identify and develop new skills requirements based on employer needs, including development of a new apprenticeship framework for the Low Carbon sector
- A talent pipeline to stimulate the supply of the future workforce, including business engagement across schools on STEM based initiatives, colleges and universities to encourage careers within the Low Carbon sector
- Pre-employment pathways to enable employers to shape recruitment programmes and voluntary class/work based training initiatives aimed to increase the job readiness and take up of entry level employment
- The development of Independent Skills Advisors to engage SMEs and identify skills needs linked to business direction, competitiveness and growth
- Business networking for SMEs to share market knowledge, excellence in skills and training investment, engagement with research and development to drive product innovation and linkages to business support initiatives.

Work with employers on skills utilisation and productivity

Skills utilisation approaches look at how the workforce is structured and the relationship between an individual's skills and the needs of business. Skills utilisation approaches focus on how well employers are utilising the skills of their employees, which can improve productivity and profitability. Individuals also gain from the better utilisation of their skills through greater job satisfaction and autonomy. This approach avoids supply-side or "provider driven" training solutions, which may not address the breadth of an enterprise's organisational context. Instead, providers are encouraged to take on a workforce development role (Froy, Giguère and Meghnagi, 2012).

Although Employer Ownership pilot projects and Union Learning representative activities are associated with promoting job quality and enhancing skills utilisation, improving work organisation has not been a prime focus of local public sector activity in England. Indeed, in Hull while interviewees recognised the importance of decent work, they indicated that the key issue was ensuring that people were able to access work. In general, participants in the local roundtables agreed with the general laissez-fare approach to internal organisation of work and the utilisation of skills, which are considered the responsibility of employers.

Nevertheless, mentoring and knowledge sharing activities – which may be formal or informal events relying on serendipity – fall under this general heading. Such activities were considered to be very important at BioCity (a bioscience incubator) in Nottingham (see Box 3.13 for further details). One of the advantages of having a cluster of bioscience companies was stated to be "peer-to-peer support" in "upping knowledge". Likewise, activities relating to employer ownership of skills may be helpful in raising awareness on issues, such as quality jobs and skills utilisation.

Box 3.13. **BioCity and MediCity: the life sciences sector in Nottingham**

BioCity was established in Nottingham in 2002-03. It specialises in the creation and development of business incubation sites for the life sciences. It provides a home for new and growing businesses and creates the right environment for tenant companies to have the strongest chance of success. BioCity provides laboratory and office facilities on a flexible basis and access to high-end equipment, shared services, training, business support and access to investment.

MediCity is a joint venture between Alliance Boots, and BioCity. MediCity aims to provide a stimulating and supportive business development environment for innovators in consumer healthcare, medical technology, diagnostics, and beauty products. MediCity is based within the Nottingham Enterprise Zone on the Boots site in Beeston. The idea is that businesses housed at MediCity will benefit from BioCity's experience of growing successful businesses in specialised incubator environments and Alliance Boots expertise in the global healthcare market.

Research on the theme of work organisation has been taken forward at Nottingham Trent University and an initiative to improve management and leadership skills was funded by the former Regional Development Agency EMDA in 2009-10. The "Innovative Workplaces" project (IWP), managed and delivered by Acas (Advisory, Conciliation and Arbitration Service), with the UK Work Organisation Network (UKWON) as the delivery partner, offered in-depth support to ten diverse organisations seeking to improve organisational performance. The IWP set out to stimulate organisational change, to be workplace-focused, to provide customised organisational support and to develop managerial and leadership skills through a practical approach. The IWP offered direct support to two nominated representatives from each of the ten participating organisations.

The underlying rationale was that a handful of key individuals could successfully be the catalyst for sustainable organisational change. The evaluation evidence revealed that the IWP led to improvements in the participating organisations in the areas of workplace communications, and employee involvement and engagement (Harris et al., 2011). The economic impact assessment of the IWP reported an overall minimum return on investment of GBP 4 for every GBP 1 of public sector expenditure. However, around a third of participants felt that without the IWP, the momentum for change would not be sustained.

Involvement of education and training institutions in local applied research

Local universities and colleges in all case study areas are active in applied research. While some of this research serves national markets, other research is applied locally. One example is the link between BioCity and life sciences at the University of Nottingham and the Queens Medical Centre. Another example from Nottingham is the work of the Economic Strategy Research Bureau at Nottingham Trent University, which houses strategic research expertise from EMDA and is one of a number of applied research centres providing educational courses and research and consultancy support to local businesses. In Hull, the Business School and other parts of the University are active in applied research; for example a pan-university team undertook a strategic review of clusters in the sub-region, feeding into the LEP strategic planning process. Other studies include a "White Paper" on the Humber's future economic and sustainable development[15] and research into internationalisation activities among Humber SMEs.

The funding model of higher and further education institutions in England means that support often has to be provided at cost (rather than being made available free of charge) – unless external funding can be generated to support the research.

Promotion of skills for entrepreneurship

Entrepreneurship training and VET

In England a strong emphasis has been placed on promoting skills for entrepreneurship and enhancing awareness of self-employment as a possible route into employment. For those who are not in employment the PES, private and third sector organisations all promote entrepreneurship. Nationally, the New Enterprise Allowance, launched in 2011, can provide money and mentoring support to help people start their own business if they get certain benefits and have a business idea that could work.

Likewise, further education colleges in the case study areas are active in the enterprise agenda and integrate entrepreneurship into many or all of their programmes. New College Nottingham is part of the Gazelle Colleges Group which is a leader on the entrepreneurship agenda,[16] highlighting the importance of developing an "entrepreneurial mindset" (encompassing being confident, innovative, resilient, enterprise-aware and willing to "have a go") – amongst their students in order to prepare them for personal, social and economic success and seeking to foster a new generation of entrepreneurs through harnessing the experience and expertise of successful entrepreneurs (locally and nationally).

Hull has a relatively low position on the "league table" of business start-ups, as indicated for example by the Centre for Cities' "Small Business Outlook" series (Centre for Cities, 2014). The most recent report indicates that existing Hull SMEs are becoming more growth-orientated than previously, but the city ranks 61st out of 64 cities in terms of the concentration of SMEs per 10 000 population and 59th in relation to the rate of business start-up. This situation has persisted for many years in Hull. The factors underpinning low levels of entrepreneurial activity in areas such as Hull are complex,[17] but interviewees for this project highlighted the city's industrial past (associated with large employers and low-level skills), relatively low levels of income and wealth and historically limited investment in entrepreneurial education.

As a result of these relatively low indicators of entrepreneurial activity and increasing recognition of the importance of SMEs to economic development, a range of organisations in Hull have been active in promoting entrepreneurship, especially among young people. Hull City Council is regarded as one of the leading authorities in England with regard to the promotion of youth entrepreneurship in schools, colleges working closely with Rotherham (in South Yorkshire) and Leeds City Region. In Hull, while most interviewees recognised the importance and significance of entrepreneurship, some expressed the view that enterprise education is not a high priority of the Humber LEP and more should be done.

The York, North Yorkshire and East Riding LEP, which incorporates Scarborough, places considerable emphasis on entrepreneurship and SME development as drivers of local economic growth. The chair of the LEP is a SME owner from the Scarborough district and the LEP Strategic Economic Plan places considerable emphasis on the role of the LEP in supporting 'business inspired growth.'

Entrepreneurship training within universities

At university level, entrepreneurship is promoted amongst students and enterprise awareness is embedded across the curriculum, but the prominence given varies by discipline – such that it may be afforded a higher profile in business related and creative design courses. There is a well-developed programme at The Hive at Nottingham Trent University, which is a purpose-built centre for entrepreneurship and enterprise (see Box 3.14).

Box 3.14. **The Hive, Nottingham Trent University**

The Hive supports the creation of new businesses as well as fostering the delivery of entrepreneurship education into the curriculum across the University. It is primarily for students and graduates at the University, but it is also open to other business ideas that will benefit from association with the University. The Hive provides:

- Business support services, including training programmes, mentoring and general guidance and advice.
- First-class office facilities.
- Access to invaluable information services and relevant organisations.
- Competitively priced office accommodation.
- Access to funding opportunities, grants and useful events.
- Access to networking opportunities.
- Mentoring support.

Support is organised such that businesses can "start fast, grow fast and fail fast." Since 2011, The Hive as helped more than 250 start-up companies, of which more 70% are still trading. Many of these are in the Creative sector and in IT.

There is an associated outreach project in North Nottinghamshire called *Hive@Mansfield*. It helps would-be entrepreneurs to research and evaluate their ideas and assist in the development of a business plan and associated business skills. Hive@Mansfield is open to anyone with a business idea, and tends to attract an older age profile of would-be entrepreneurs than The Hive at Nottingham, including some "reluctant entrepreneurs" who have turned to thinking of setting up a business in the absence of other opportunities for employment. Core funding for The Hive is from Higher Education Innovation Funding (HEIF), and this funding is used to leverage further funding.

The Hive and Nottingham Trent University collaborate with the University of Nottingham, New College Nottingham and Central College Nottingham on *Inspired in Nottingham* which is designed to create opportunities for students and graduates aged up to 35 years old to set up businesses and encourage graduates to stay in Nottingham after their studies. The idea is that the *Inspired in Nottingham* team will match the needs of young entrepreneurs with relevant local businesses that have the necessary skills and experience.

The commitment to entrepreneurship in Nottingham is highlighted by the fact that *Inspired in Nottingham* is part of the Nottingham City Deal *Generation Y* programme which is targeted at young people aged between 16-35 years, and provides advice, support and training to give people the ability and confidence to start their own business. The Government is working with Nottingham as a pilot area for start-up loans for young entrepreneurs and is making up to GBP 1 million available for start-up accelerator programmes for young entrepreneurs. Nottingham City Council is investing GBP 0.3 million in the support programme and a fund of GBP 0.7 million for small scale capital investment/refurbishment loans for young entrepreneurs in the Creative Quarter.

Likewise, the University of Hull (which is the only higher education institution in Hull and the Humber sub-region) is active in promoting entrepreneurship among its students. The University's Enterprise Centre provides a focal point for this activity along with the Business School, although all faculties have leaders responsible for enterprise and run programmes to stimulate entrepreneurial skills among the students. Recent and current activities include:

- Graduate Enterprise Programmes, supported by the European Regional Development Fund and delivered in partnership with other universities across Yorkshire and the Humber. This provides financial and mentoring support for aspiring student and graduate entrepreneurs, including an annual regional "boot camp"
- *Incubator units* in the Enterprise Centre and the Business School: these are available to all types of businesses but are often used by student and graduate entrepreneurs
- *Student Enterprise Society*, run by the Students Union with support from University staff
- *"Starting a New Business"*: a module for undergraduate students run by the Business School but available to all Hull University students. This entails students working in teams to develop business ideas and plans, which are then presented to staff members and business people and assessed as part of the students' degrees.

Economic development promotes quality jobs for local people

Inward investment strategies focus on skills and quality jobs

Information on the local area is made available to inward investors. This includes information on skills but also on the physical infrastructure – including broadband and transport links. However, several interviewees in Nottingham and North Nottinghamshire highlighted that inward investment could provide only a small proportion of jobs growth in the future. Interviewees tended to think that the primary focus of economic development was on the "quantity" of jobs, with the "quality" of jobs as a secondary focus. There were also some concerns that inward investment strategies in Nottingham and North Nottinghamshire might focus on "low costs" (relative to centres such as London) and so reinforce concerns about a "low skills equilibrium".

For Hull, the most significant inward investment activity has been the decision of Siemens to locate an assembly facility for offshore wind turbines in the city, with the likely creation of 1 200 jobs directly and many more indirectly, through supply chain and multiplier impacts. The development of the site is due to commence in 2014 and the manufacturing facility will be fully operational by 2017. In addition, it is likely that 350 jobs will be created as a result of a proposed investment by Korean wind tower manufacturer CS Wind Corporation. These developments were in the early stages at the time of writing, but all indications are that Siemens and associated developments are likely to create relatively high-skilled highly-paid jobs requiring STEM skills (engineering in particular) and local agencies – led by the LEP – are working to ensure that the local VET sector is geared up to provide these skills and that young people in the area are aware of the potential opportunities and the skills and qualifications that they will need to take advantage of them.

It is important to note that Hull and the Humber are not the only potential beneficiaries of the Siemens and associated "green energy" investments in the area. It is anticipated that the east coast of England will be an important base for supplies, maintenance, transport and other services associated with the large wind energy facility that is being developed in the North Sea. Partners in Scarborough district, for example, have identified the potential for local businesses to provide marine transport services to support those working on the offshore wind turbine facility.

Quality local jobs are sourced through new local developments and public procurement

As far as possible, employment and training opportunities are sought through local construction and development activities. In construction, this tends to be done through "Section 106 agreements" (i.e. agreements between developers and local planning authorities that are negotiated as part of a condition of planning consent).

In Nottingham, via Section 106 agreements, developers are required to use the Employer Hub for their recruitment and training, thus prioritising local residents, for all developments of over ten houses. UK and EU frameworks support the inclusion of social and community benefits in public procurement, provided this does not disadvantage non-local bidders. There is growing recognition that targeted recruitment and training opportunities in public contracts can help to address issues of poverty, non-employment and a lack of social mobility. In Nottingham local employment requirements are considered for all contracts over GBP 200 000. Yet some interviewees felt that procurement had been under-utilised to date – partly because of concerns about procurement regulations. Looking ahead, major investment in HS2 (a high speed rail line with a planned interchange in the East Midlands) offers an opportunity for upskilling in the construction and engineering sectors.

Theme 4: Being inclusive

Figure 3.5. **Dashboard Results: Being inclusive**

Sub-Criteria

4.1 Employment and training programmes are geared to local "at-risk" groups

4.2 Childcare and family friendly policies to support women's participation in employment

4.3 Tackling youth unemployment

4.4 Openness to immigration

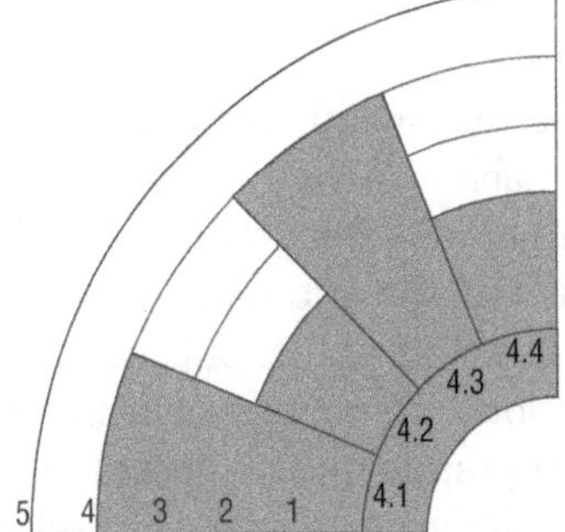

Employment and training programmes are geared to local "at-risk" groups

Various groups have been identified as "at risk" at the national level. These are disabled people, lone parents, ethnic minorities, people aged 50 and over, those with no qualifications and those living in the most deprived local authority wards. In Nottingham, there are specific targets to reduce the unemployment rates amongst the Black British group and those in the Mixed ethnic group who suffer disproportionately high unemployment. Nottingham has also been a pioneer as an "Early Intervention City" with a series of interventions to break the 0–18 cycle of dysfunction. In Hull, almost all interviewees pinpointed the information, advice and guidance (IAG) system in schools as a weak point that needed improving in order to ensure that young people are guided to get skills and qualifications that are relevant to the labour market. It was noted that it is also important to educate parents.

Recent attention has focused specifically on young people not in employment, education or training (NEET). In Hull especially, NEETs were the main "at risk" group identified by interviewees. In Nottingham, activity has focused on implementation of the Nottingham City Employer Hub and the Apprenticeships Hub, with work undertaken in neighbourhoods, through schools, FE colleges and the community/voluntary sectors. The PES is also active in working in partnership to conduct outreach activities in disadvantaged areas. While outreach activity is tailored to engaging particular groups and some assistance with transport is available to help people take advantage of opportunities, in general VET and adult training programmes are not geared specifically to the needs of "at risk" groups. In Hull, the Humber Learning Consortium oversees a wide range of initiatives to address the needs of "at risk" groups, working with voluntary and community groups. In Scarborough, residents of those neighbourhoods featured in the higher levels of the Index of Multiple Deprivation are the primary focus of inclusion-related initiatives.

A relatively new focus of intervention is the family (as opposed to the individual) following the launch of the national "Troubled Families" programme. In Nottingham City, the focus is on Priority Families which have complex needs – i.e. households who have at least two of the following: *(1)* problems with crime and anti-social behaviour, *(2)* children not in school and *(3)* an adult on out-of-work benefits. The rationale underlying this approach is that tackling one problem alone is not going to work in the long-term. Rather, it is better to support and engage with every member of the family in a partnership approach.

Childcare and family friendly policies to support women's participation in employment

Issues of childcare and family friendly policies to support women's participation in employment did not feature strongly in discussions with stakeholders, beyond the provision of childcare facilities for people participating in Jobcentre Plus or Work Programme activities.

Some interviewees mentioned that previously, the Sure Start programme initiated by the previous UK Labour Government, was concerned with supporting children, parents and communities through the integration of early education, childcare and health and family support services. The specific focus was on disadvantaged areas, to ensure that children got the best possible start in life. Subsequently, the provision of Children's Centres to meet the needs of the local community became a statutory requirement for local authorities. The Sure Start programme was subject to extensive and intensive local evaluation (www.ness.bbk.ac.uk/) with mixed findings in relation to their impact on families. However, an economic analysis pointed to some positive effects in relation to the future life prospects of children in families participating in the programme (Meadows, 2011). National funding for Sure Start was discontinued in 2012, with freedom available to local areas to fund similar provision if they so wished. Recognising a continuing need for childcare, Hull City Council has continued to support a number of Children's Centres that were originally set up as Sure Start centres. More generally, interviewees noted that childcare was an issue for some people in accessing employment, but other specific local initiatives were not identified.

Tackling youth unemployment

As noted above, tackling youth unemployment is a key focus of activity, with several recent and current policy initiatives seeking to address this issue.

Several interviewees mentioned the Future Jobs Fund (FJF), introduced in parts of England with high levels of worklessness in October 2009 to support the creation of subsidised jobs for unemployed people who were at a disadvantage in the labour market. The FJF was primarily aimed at 18-24-year-olds in receipt of Jobseeker's Allowance (JSA). Nottingham's FJF placed 1 000 people into paid work for a year. Over 30% of those who benefited from the scheme were taken on full-time by their employers at the end of their placement. The FJF was terminated by the UK Coalition Government. Estimates suggest that FJF had a net cost to the Exchequer of approximately GBP 3 100 per participant and created net benefits to participants of approximately GBP 4 000 per participant, to employers of approximately GBP 6 850 per participant and to society of approximately GBP 7 750 per participant (DWP, 2012). An independent evaluation of FJF indicates that the six-month job placements under the initiative were considered by both participants and employers to be long enough to raise employability and provide a gateway into the open labour market for some participants (Fishwick et al., 2011). What participants valued especially was having a "real job" with an employer and time to prove themselves with that employer. This was endorsed by interviewees, several of whom felt that the learning point about "real jobs" should be embedded in future initiatives.

Since 2011, the *Nottingham Jobs Fund* has been operating in Nottingham. The Nottingham Jobs Fund offers a salary subsidy of 50% of the minimum wage for a year to an employer if they take an unemployed Nottingham City resident who is 18 years or over. To be eligible for the wage subsidy, the job in question must be additional to the existing structure of the company/organisation, be guaranteed for 6-12 months, be for 30 hours per week, pay at least the National Minimum Wage and have the potential to become a sustainable job after the placement period.

In Hull, Springboard is the flagship NEET programme funded through the LEP and delivered by City Works (see Box 3.15). This is an innovative programme that tries to engage young people who have been disaffected by school.

Box 3.15. **Hull Springboard programme**

The Hull Springboard programme, targeted at NEETs across the city, is funded through the Humber learning Consortium and delivered by City Works. A key feature of the programme is that it contains no classroom-type teaching, in recognition of the fact that many NEET young people feel alienated from formal education as a result of their experiences at school or college. Instead, the programme organises a wide range of activities, including trips (a recent one was to London) designed to help young people improve their confidence, social and employability skills and to learn without necessarily sitting in a classroom. For example, the participants are encouraged to discuss and debate issues arising from reading newspaper or internet articles.

Under the Humber City Deal, a further GBP 1.5 million will be invested in the Springboard programme, focused on encouraging and supporting young people to take up apprenticeships and introducing a personalised budget for young people to enable them to secure the support they need to get into work or training.

Another initiative to tackle NEETs – especially so-called "hidden NEETs" – is *Talent Match*. This programme, funded by the Big Lottery Fund, is operational from 2014 in 21 LEP areas in England, including in Hull and Nottingham. In Hull, the initiative is led by the Humber Learning Consortium. In Nottingham and North Nottinghamshire, the Greater Nottingham Goundwork Trust has been awarded a Talent Match grant over five years to fund activity which is tackling 27 hot spots of high unemployment across the D2N2 LEP area.

Co-creation is a key principle of Talent Match in all local areas, with young people playing a key role in designing interventions that meet their needs and aspirations as they move towards developing their skills and employment. Young people are also involved in commissioning of services. Some young people will also be employed to deliver services to other young people.

Each of the 21 Talent Match partnerships in England is led by a voluntary sector organisation. In the D2N2 LEP area, Greater Nottingham Groundwork works in a cross-sector partnership also involving the public sector, private sector employers and other voluntary organisations. The emphasis is on needs-led person-centred solutions and intensive mentoring. Specific outcomes of the programme are: *(1)* improved emotional capabilities and attitudes, *(2)* improved interpersonal skills, *(3)* successfully overcoming practical barriers, *(4)* gaining qualifications, skills and expertise, *(5)* improved skills for finding and sustaining work, *(6)* gaining and sustaining employment and enterprise and *(7)* developing effective employer engagement with young people.

While interviewees agreed that addressing NEETs is an important policy priority and that partnership working was essential, some concerns were raised about the potential for duplication of activity amongst organisations working with NEETs and for double or triple counting of outcomes when two or more organisations worked with the same young person. One view put forward was that given their size and resources, it is appropriate for local authorities to take a lead role in co-ordinating and brokering relationships and that what might be thought of as excessive competition for the same people (in this case NEETs) might be counterproductive. This raises the question of whether there can be too much activity and overly complex partnership working that is unlikely to be checked given that it is in the interests of individual organisations to bid for available contracts/grants.

Openness to immigration

Immigration is a key issue in national political debate in England and it has greater prominence in some local areas than in others. The relatively low score in the framework on this issue mainly reflects a lack of strategic emphasis on local policy initiatives targeted specifically at immigrants at the time of the interviews, especially vis-à-vis issues such as youth unemployment.

Over the last decade, Nottingham and North Nottinghamshire, in common with other local areas in England, have seen a large inflow of migrants, mainly from countries in Eastern and Central Europe that joined the EU in 2004 and 2007. Nottingham has a longer history of immigration. There was a wave of migration to the city from the Caribbean in the 1950s. According to the 2011 Census of Population, nearly 36% of the population of Nottingham was from non-White British ethnic groups. 13% of the population was from Asian British groups, 7% from Black groups, 6% from Mixed groups and 5% from Other White groups. In North Nottinghamshire, the proportion of the population of White British origin is higher than in Nottingham and the largest single minority group is the Other White group (including people from Eastern and Central Europe).

Neither Hull nor Scarborough has a history of mass immigration, so it is unsurprising that ethnicity/immigration has not played a major role in skills and employment policies, beyond a general commitment to equal opportunities. However, there have also been influxes of Eastern and Central European migrants. For the most part these groups are not felt to have particular needs in relation to skills and training; indeed the prevailing view seemed to be that these migrants are well-qualified (even if working in jobs requiring only low skills levels) and often entrepreneurial.

Whereas people from other EU Member States have the right to enter the UK as "free movers", migrants from third countries are now subject to the Points Based System, which focuses on highly skilled migrants who can meet skill shortages and skills gaps in the UK. These migrants are unlikely to have specific skills needs and those that they do have are most likely addressed by employers. Support for migrants for recognition of qualifications gained abroad is not automatically available from the PES or from local authorities. Rather migrants can seek advice from UK NARIC: the National Agency responsible for providing information, advice and expert opinion on the comparability of qualifications worldwide. This is a service that the individual has to pay for. Likewise, employers can also seek support from NARIC. There are not specific courses geared towards immigrants entering the labour market, although employers could pay for courses if they wish to do so.

It is recognised that English language ability is central to finding a decent job and progressing in work in the UK. For many migrants, the first priority is finding a job. Difficulties in finding information about suitable English language provision, the cost of provision, the sometimes inconvenient location of provision, time, lack of care support and lack of encouragement may act as barriers to taking up English language learning. Because of difficulties in conversion of qualifications to the UK system and/or barriers to taking up English language learning, some migrants may be working in jobs below their qualification levels and/or in sectors and occupations where migrant workers predominate (as was mentioned in relation to warehousing in parts of North Nottinghamshire). There were some indications in the local case study areas of pressure on English language learning provision.

ESOL (English for Speakers of Other Languages) providers may find themselves having to cope with an extremely diverse intake of ESOL learners, from those who are highly educated and proficient learners tackling a new language to those who are not literate in their own languages. This poses challenges to fundamental concepts in qualification and learning systems, such as an "average learner" and an "average time taken", which are taken as a basis for calculating funding. Since 2008, eligibility for free ESOL provision has become increasingly restricted. From 2011/12 only benefit claimants looking for work have been entitled to fee remission on ESOL classes. Some providers have responded by switching ESOL into functional skills provision. Immigrants may be covered by this or have to rely on informal provision. Employers may choose to fund English language learning for their workers.

Public sector organisations and not-for-profit organisations seek to ensure that there is no discrimination in the workplace, but actions tend to be ad hoc. At the local level, Citizens Advice is in a position to monitor issues regarding pay and any other aspects of discrimination raised by people going to them for advice, and then making these issues more widely known. At national level, the Home Office and Migration Advisory Committee (MAC) have sponsored research on the experience of migrants in the labour market, as have some local authorities (Migration Advisory Committee, 2014; Green et al., 2014).

Notes

1. The Big Lottery Fund awards lottery money to community groups and projects.

2. All children in England aged 5-16 years are entitled to a free place at a state school. Most state schools have to follow the National Curriculum.

3. Academies are publicly funded independent schools; money comes direct from government (not the local council). They are run by an academy trust which employs the staff. Some academies have sponsors (e.g. businesses, universities, other schools, faith groups, etc) who are responsible for improving performance of the school. They do not have to follow the National Curriculum.

4. Free schools are funded by the government but are not run by the local council. They have greater freedom than state schools; they do not have to follow the National Curriculum. Free schools are run on a not-for-profit basis and can be set up by charities, universities, communities and faith groups, teachers, parents, businesses, etc.

5. UTCs are a type of free school providing a technical education (e.g. in engineering) alongside study of academic subjects, typically for 14-19 year olds.

6. Studio schools are a type of free school. They are small (usually with around 300 pupils). They deliver mainstream qualifications through project-based learning. Students work with local employers and a personal coach, and follow a curriculum designed to give them skills and qualifications needed for work or to take up further education.

7. Private schools (also known as independent schools) are not administered by government and are funded wholly or partly by charging for their students' tuition.

8. FE Colleges offer any study after compulsory secondary education that is not part of higher education (i.e. is not taken as part of an undergraduate or graduate degree).

9. The SFA funds skills training for further education (FE) in England.

10. The Learning and Skills Council was responsible for funding and planning education and training for over 16-year-olds in England until March 2010.

11. Statutory bodies, executive agencies, NDPBs, etc.

12. www.hlc-vol.org/ (accessed 20 July 2014).

13. Note that Scarborough District is part of the York, North Yorkshire and East Riding LEP, not the Humber LEP with which Hull is affiliated.

14. https://www.gov.uk/government/uploads/system/uploads/attachment_data/file/305174/lmi-for-all-flyer-5.pdf (accessed 20 July 2014).

15. www2.hull.ac.uk/pdf/HumberFutureEcoSustainDevReport_April2013.pdf (accessed 20 July 2014).

16. See www.gazellecolleges.com/about-us (accessed 20 July 2014).

17. See, for example Fotopoulos, G. (2014), "On the spatial stickiness of UK new firm formation rates", *Journal of Economic Geography*, 14(3) 651-679, Oxford Journal, Oxford.

References

Andrews, D. (2013), *The future of careers work in schools in England: what are the options? – A discussion paper,* www.thecdi.net/write/the_future_of_careers_work_in_schools_in_england__march_2013.pdf (accessed 25 July 2014).

Centre for Cities (2014), *Small Business Outlook,* www.centreforcities.org/assets/files/2014/14-06-18-Small-Business-Outlook.pdf (accessed 25 July 2014).

Chartered Institute of Personnel and Development (CIPD) (2013), *Employers are from Mars, Young People are from Venus: Addressing the Young People/Jobs Mismatch,* CIPD, London.

Department of Work and Pensions (DWP) (2012), *Impacts and Costs and Benefits of the Future Jobs Fund,* DWP, London, https://www.gov.uk/government/uploads/system/uploads/attachment_data/file/223120/impacts_costs_benefits_fjf.pdf.

Fishwick T., P. Lane and L. Gardiner (2011), *Future Jobs Fund: An Independent National Evaluation,* Centre for Economic and Social Inclusion, London.

Fotopoulos, G. (2014), "On the spatial stickiness of UK new firm formation rates", *Journal of Economic Geography,* 14(3) 651-679.

Froy, F., S. Giguère and M. Meghnagi (2012), *Skills for Competitiveness: A Synthesis Report,* OECD Local Economic and Employment Development (LEED) Working Papers, No. 2012/09, OECD Publishing, Paris, http://dx.doi.org/10.1787/5k98xwskmvr6-en.

Green, A.E. et al. (2014), *Determinants of the composition of the workforce in low skilled sectors of the UK economy: social care and retail sectors,* Institute for Employment Research, University of Warwick, Coventry, https://www.gov.uk/government/uploads/system/uploads/attachment_data/file/333083/MAC-Migrants_in_low-skilled_work__Full_report_2014.pdf (accessed 25 July 2014).

Harris, L. et al. (2011), *Unlocking Engagement: A Review of the 'Innovative Workplaces' Initiative,* ACAS, London.

House of Commons Work and Pensions Committee (2014), "The role of Jobcentre Plus in the reformed welfare system", Second Report of Session 2013-14, The Stationery Office, London.

Hutchinson, J. and B. Dickinson (2014), "Employers and schools: How Mansfield is building a world of work approach", *Local Economy* 29, 257-266, London.

Meadows, P. (2011), *National Evaluation of Sure Start Local Programmes: An Economic Perspective,* Department for Education, Research Report DFE-RR073, London.

McCoshan, A. and J. Hillage (2013), *OECD Review: Skills Beyond School. Background Report for England,* UKCES, Wath-upon-Dearne and London.

Migration Advisory Committee (2014), *Migrants in low-skilled work: The growth of EU and non-EU labour in low-skilled jobs and its impact on the UK,* Migration Advisory Committee, London, https://www.gov.uk/government/uploads/system/uploads/attachment_data/file/333083/MAC-Migrants_in_low-skilled_work__Full_report_2014.pdf (accessed 25 July 2014).

Mosley, H., H. Schütz and N. Breyer (2001), "Management by Objectives in European Public Employment Services", *Discussion Paper* FSI01-203, Social Science Research Centre (WZB), Berlin.

National Careers Council (2014), *Taking action: Achieving a culture change in careers provision,* National Careers Council, London, https://www.gov.uk/government/uploads/system/uploads/attachment_data/file/355473/bis-14-1080-taking-action-achieving-a-culture-change-in-careers-provision.pdf (accessed 25 July 2014).

National Careers Council (2013), *An Aspirational Nation: Creating a culture change in careers provision*, National Careers Council, London, https://www.gov.uk/government/uploads/system/uploads/attachment_data/file/354644/bis-13-919-national-careers-council-report-an-aspirational-nation-creating-a-culture-change-in-careers-provison.pdf (accessed 25 July 2014).

OECD (2014a), *Job Creation and Local Economic Development*, OECD Publishing, Paris, http://dx.doi.org/10.1787/9789264215009-en.

OECD (2014b), *Connecting People with Jobs: Activation Policies in the United Kingdom*, OECD Publishing, Paris, http://dx.doi.org/10.1787/9789264217188-en.

Office for Standards in Education, Children's Services and Skills (Ofsted) (2013), *Going in the Right Direction? Careers Guidance in Schools from September 2012*, Ofsted, London.

Witty, A. (2013), *Encouraging a British Invention Revolution: Sir Andrew Witty's Review of Universities and Growth,* UK Government, London, https://www.gov.uk/government/uploads/system/uploads/attachment_data/file/249720/bis-13-1241-encouraging-a-british-invention-revolution-andrew-witty-review-R1.pdf (accessed 25 July 2014).

Chapter 4

Towards an action plan for jobs in England: Recommendations and best practices

Stimulating job creation at the local level requires integrated actions across employment, training, and economic development portfolios. Co-ordinated place-based policies can help workers find suitable jobs, while also contributing to demand by stimulating productivity. This requires flexible policy management frameworks, information, and integrated partnerships which leverage the efforts of local stakeholders. This chapter outlines the key recommendations emerging from the review of local job creation policies in England.

This report has highlighted a large number of initiatives, projects and programmes that are in operation in the four local case study areas in England attempting to address employment and skills challenges. While each area has its own specific structures and in some cases bespoke initiatives designed to address specific developments (e.g. wind energy in Hull), there is considerable potential for sharing of lessons between the different areas. National agencies might consider whether some of the initiatives and approaches described in this report might be scaled up to the national level to address many of the issues that are common to most areas, most notably the need to engage employers more deeply in employability and skills development activities. This chapter highlights the main recommendations emerging from this review of local job creation policies in England.

Better aligning programmes and policies to local economic development

Recommendation: Ensure that local governance structures such as the Local Enterprise Partnerships are "fit for purpose" in terms of the geographical levels at which they operate and the strategic public/private leadership that they engender, while ensuring that they link effectively to national government actors.

Findings from the in-depth analysis undertaken for this study suggest that local areas in England are still in a period of transition from a relatively well-funded system of Regional Development Agencies that had mixed impacts to a more localised business-led approach focused around Local Enterprise Partnerships. There are potential benefits from such an approach, especially in relation to facilitating the strategic engagement and input of local employers into decisions regarding employment and skills provision, but there are capacity constraints. At the local level, there is a need and a desire for a clear "local centre of gravity" as a central hub within a fragmented system. Local Enterprise Partnerships are well positioned to play this role but there is a need to acknowledge the position of local authorities who are democratically accountable and significant actors in terms of resources and expertise.

It is too early to evaluate the success of the Local Enterprise Partnerships in terms of increasing the role of the local level in leading employment and training policies. Following a period of rapid change in institutional architecture in England, there was a clear consensus from stakeholders in the case study areas that it was important to avoid any further significant institutional changes in the local economic development, employment and skills system and consolidate on the basis of existing architecture. Therefore, it is recommended that the Government works to ensure the long-term stability of the economic development institutional structures in England. This includes undertaking active monitoring to review their remit and geography, and their effectiveness in ensuring that local providers respond rapidly and effectively to changing employment and skills needs, given their importance for partnership working and policy delivery at the city-region/local level. This will facilitate better local policy integration and coherence between economic development, employment and skills actors, In theory, some rationalisation of Local Enterprise Partnership boundaries might be appropriate (e.g. to eliminate cases where districts are in two LEP areas) and it is possible to make a case for boundaries to more fully reflect travel-to-work areas, but practically there are advantages of retaining most of the current boundaries and ensuring that local authority districts nest within current Local Enterprise Partnership areas.

Recommendation: Facilitate the further decentralisation of funding for skills programmes. Review funding arrangements associated with the Skills Funding Agency to allow greater flexibility to meet employer and learner needs at the local level

Despite the trend towards the localisation of powers regarding employment and skills policies, the majority of programmes to help unemployed people into work continue to be delivered and/or financed by DWP. This includes the flagship national Work Programme, which is organised around regional contracts with approved primary contractors, albeit with some delivery by local agencies that have limited flexibility within sub-contracts. While some flexibility exists for local Jobcentre Plus managers to target funds on priority groups or types of provision, these flexibilities are operational rather than strategic; hence the overall picture continues to be one of relative centralisation of most DWP provision.

It is recommended that the Government facilitates the further decentralisation of funding for and provision of DWP programmes to ensure greater responsiveness to the needs of job-seekers and/or local employers. When the current Work Programme contracts end, there is scope to reform the contractual arrangements for the Work Programme to bring its planning and delivery closer to the needs of local areas such as the ones reviewed in this study. In particular, it would be beneficial for local actors to have greater influence over the Work Programme (and its successors), with access to data disaggregated to local areas to help inform policy development at the local level (OECD, 2014a).

The picture in relation to the responsiveness of the vocational training sector is mixed. While there have been moves towards decentralisation and there are examples of locally-focused provision linked to employer needs, there is still scope to ensure that the further education sector is enabled to be more responsive to local needs. Strategically, there is a role here for the Local Enterprise Partnerships to ensure that provision is meeting the needs of employers. It is recommended that a review be undertaken of the funding arrangements associated with the Skills Funding Agency to find ways of enabling funding of "bite-sized" provision, which is more suitable for smaller employers and will also ensure flexible responses to labour market shocks. More flexible provision will also reduce programme and policies rigidities that stall new innovative practices and better accord with the direction of travel on the Employer Ownership of Skills agenda.

Box 4.1. **Policy tools and mechanisms for injecting greater strategic flexibility into the employment and skills system**

Allocating more flexibility requires that local actors take more responsibility in the design and delivery of employment and skills policies. OECD research has identified the following ways of injecting flexibility at the local level:

Programme design: Do sub-regional offices have any input into the design of policies and programmes? Are they consulted? Can they influence the programme mix and adapt design features of programmes, including target groups, or are these largely centrally determined? May local Public Employment Service (PES) offices implement programmes outside the standard programme portfolio? Do they design local employment strategies?

Financing: Do sub-regional actors have flexible global budgets or line item budgets for active measures? To what extent can they allocate resources flexibly between budget items for active measures?

Box 4.1. **Policy tools and mechanisms for injecting greater strategic flexibility into the employment and skills system** *(continued)*

Target groups: Can local offices decide on the target groups for their assistance locally or do programmes already specify particular target groups?

Goals and performance management: To what extent are organisational goals and targets centrally determined? Do they allow room for sub-regional goals and hence flexibility in adapting goals to local circumstances? Are targets and indicators hierarchically imposed or negotiated with regional and local actors and harmonised with broader local economic strategies? Is performance assessment based solely on quantitative criteria?

Collaboration: Are local offices free to participate in partnerships, and do they collaborate with other actors? Can local offices decide who they collaborate with locally?

Outsourcing: Are local offices responsible for outsourcing services to external providers? Can they influence the terms of reference of contracts with service providers?

Source: Giguère, S. and F. Froy (eds.) (2009), *Flexible Policy for More and Better Jobs*, Local Economic and Employment Development (LEED), OECD Publishing, Paris, http://dx.doi.org/10.1787/9789264059528-en.

Recommendation: Reinforce the stability of the employment and skills system locally by ensuring that funding and governance arrangements strike an optimal balance between competition and cooperation

While there are some instances of limited accessibility to the employment and skills system (e.g. in rural areas where learners may face less choice), most individuals have good access to skills development and upgrading opportunities in England. Furthermore, mechanisms have been created – for example the University Technical Colleges (UTCs), which enable new capacity to be created to respond to local needs. Going forward, it will be important to ensure that public sector contributions at the national level are matched by local public and private funding. More importantly, once such training and learning facilities are developed, it is important that funding and resources continue to be available to support ongoing provision and delivery by highly-qualified professionals who command the confidence of learners and employers.

Continuing engagement with employers as well as educational professionals, learners, careers guidance professionals and parents will be vital in order to embed the UTCs as key elements of the vocational education and training system in England. As with the Local Enterprise Partnerships, a period of stability in the institutional and funding environment will be vital to ensure that these institutions have the capacity to respond to local economic, employment and skill development needs. This would help to alleviate some of the negative consequences associated with "bidding for everything" under short-term funding regimes, which in turn can underline longer-term strategic planning locally.

There are many signs of improved policy co-ordination among local organisations concerned with employment, skills and economic development, including instances of "horizontal" working supporting "vertical" negotiations of specific local partners with actors at the national level. However the extent and nature of this co-operation has been affected by limited resources (notably in public sector organisations), unclear and/or overlapping responsibilities and competition (or "co-opetition") locally between organisations, such as Further Education colleges or voluntary sector bodies. The lack of a clear "centre of gravity" at the local level, other than local authorities, has perhaps been another factor in enabling such "co-opetition" to take place.

There is widespread recognition of the importance of employers in influencing local policies; not just large private employers, but public sector organisations and SMEs. Local Enterprise Partnerships are attempting to take the lead in relation to employment, skills and economic development, but power and influence tends to be spread around several organisations, including local authorities.

Given the overall policy focus of ensuring that policies are co-ordinated and integrated at appropriate spatial scales, extensive action is not needed by the central government. However, there needs to be a strong awareness of the potential impacts of national and/or European funding streams, which can promote unhealthy competition and may have a detrimental effect on the development of co-ordinated and integrated policies.

Recommendation: Ensure that analytical capacity is available at the local level to support data analysis and research capability. This could be through funding of local/sub-regional observatories (perhaps based in universities) or through secondment of statistical and analytical support from central government

Most organisations interviewed for this study stated their intention to base local policies on the best available evidence. However, there are some deficiencies in the quantity and quality of local data and deficits in terms of resources to undertake data analysis since the abolition of the RDAs and associated local or regional intelligence organisations.

It is recommended that the government consider how best to ensure that Local Enterprise Partnerships are enabled to fund and/or support evidence based decision making through greater capacity within these organisations (e.g. staff with data and analytical skills) and/or partnerships with other local organisations. One option would be for Local Enterprise Partnerships to establish observatories with partner organisations that would lead the co-ordination and analysis of data for their area to inform stronger strategic planning. From the in-depth work in the case study areas, it also seemed clear that local actors would benefit from benchmarking of local policies to those implemented in areas with similar local labour market characteristics. There was also an appetite for greater transparency about "what works" in the Work Programme, where there is a "black box", as opposed to a "glass box" approach.

The government should also resist the temptation to reduce budgets through the reduction of sample size and/or regularity of key surveys such as the Labour Force Survey and the Employer Skills Survey. DWP is one of the major "owners" of data on employment issues and sharing of such data with local partners should be encouraged. Local "big data" initiatives could also be used to promote stronger linkages between local economic development organisations and universities or research institutes.

The *OECD Reviews on Local Job Creation* have highlighted many instances where countries are relatively weak in evaluation and monitoring. Too often monitoring and evaluation appears to be overlooked and underfunded, partly due to the difficulties of conducting robust evaluations at the local level, and establishing realistic control groups and counterfactuals. National governments can help here by conducting their own evaluations at a larger scale, piloting projects in some areas and then helping to disseminate what works. The "What Works Centre" is a best practice in this area, which was established as a national "knowledge centre" in 2013 (see Box 4.2).

Box 4.2. **The What Works Centre evaluation of employment and training: main findings**

A "What Works Centre" has been established by the government of the United Kingdom to promote evidence-based policy making and evaluation at the local level. Upon its inception in 2013, it has conducted a review of over 1000 policy evaluations, evidence reviews and meta-analyses from the UK and other OECD countries. This exercise has produced the following findings:

- Many evaluations are not sufficiently robust – only 71 of the above evaluations met the required standards.
- Training has a positive impact on participant's employment and earnings in more than half of the evaluations reviewed.
- In-firm/on-the-job training programmes outperform classroom based training programmes. Employer co-design and activities that closely mirror actual jobs appear to be key design elements
- The state of the economy is not a major factor in the performance of training programmes. Programme design features appear to be more important in influencing the success of the programmes examined than macroeconomic factors.

Source: What Works Centre for Local Economic Growth (2014). "Evidence Review: Employment Training", www.whatworksgrowth.org.

Adding value through skills

Recommendation: Support schemes to enable SMEs to collaborate on apprenticeship and other types of training while monitoring and evaluating availability and success

The local case studies revealed that a wide variety of training is available through private providers, as well as the Further and Higher Education system. However, there were indications that training is still not sufficiently flexible to meet the needs of all employers, especially SMEs. There was some debate in the local case study interviews and roundtable discussions about the value of modular or "bite-sized" approaches to training, which may be suitable for some employers to meet specific needs at specific times, but do not always enable learners to acquire a sufficient platform to build a full range of skills and qualifications.

There was widespread recognition of the need for policy-makers and providers to work closely with employers on training issues. In particular, there was recognition of the importance of apprenticeships for fostering learning while earning in a workplace environment and providing vocational routes to skills development. A number of City Deals have foregrounded apprenticeship schemes and other local schemes, such as the Construction Works in Hull, appear to have been successful in raising the profile of training. However, there is still some way to go especially in relation to encouraging/ supporting SMEs to provide appropriate training and get involved in apprenticeships. Here it is important to be mindful of some concerns raised in local roundtable discussions that pushing too much responsibility towards (smaller) employers for administering apprenticeships might be counterproductive, causing employers to reduce their involvement. This suggests a need to be sensitive to how apprenticeships are promoted and supported.

SMEs are the engines of job creation however they often face different and unique barriers to accessing the employment and skills system. SMEs should be encouraged to provide more up-skilling opportunities to their staff and target them specifically at lower-skilled workers, as it is higher skilled workers who tend to participate in these training opportunities. Employers and workers have a joint role to play in this by supporting a culture of workplace learning. The *OECD reviews on Local Job Creation* have demonstrated the importance of establishing networks among employers, particularly SMEs at the local level and it can be used to mitigate some of the significant barriers faced by them in accessing and providing skills upgrading opportunities (See Box 4.3). It is important to build on strong networks that already exist and have a role to play in galvanising collaboration and incentivising employers to engage in the education and training system. Government financing can play a critical role in bringing employers together to develop training initiatives.

Box 4.3. **Fostering local networks to boosting skills development efforts within SMEs**

In Ireland, Skillnets was established in 1999 to promote and facilitate workplace training and up-skilling by SMEs. It is the largest organisation supporting workplace training in Ireland. In 2011, it had 70 operational networks through which it trained over 40 000 people for a total expenditure of EUR 25 million. It is a state-funded, enterprise-led body that co-invests with enterprises, particularly SMEs, when they co-operate in networks to identify and deliver training suited to their workforces. A network of SMEs, which are mostly sectoral or regional, is guided by a steering group of the local enterprise representatives. The steering group gives strategic direction and guidance to a network manager who co-ordinates all operational activity leading to the delivery of an agreed training plan with learning interventions suited for the member company workforces. The national programme is co-ordinated by Skillnets Ltd., who contract with all networks and provide programme support and monitoring to ensure the delivery of agreed quantitative and qualitative target outputs.

In 2011, 30 of these networks were located in Dublin, but were predominantly sectoral networks with a national remit and company membership. 25% of all Skillnets member companies and 33% of trainees were Dublin-based. Three networks were specific to the South East region (Carlow Kilkenny Skillnet, South Tipperary Skillnet and Waterford Chamber Skillnet). While Skillnets has a national impact, its influence is largely confined to SMEs which account for 94% of its 10 000 member companies. Originally set up to cater exclusively for the employed, since 2010 Skillnets has a mandate to include the provision of training for jobseekers. This happens both in an integrated manner with jobseekers attending programmes with employees, and also by focusing exclusively on the needs of jobseekers through the provision of dedicated longer-term programmes (e.g. the Jobseeker Support Programme) which includes work placements. Skillnets launched a pilot training initiative, ManagementWorks, providing management training to the SME community with a key focus on owner-managers.

Recommendation: Fill the gap in careers advice provision by further involving employers in the education system

For benefit claimants, Jobcentre Plus promotes the use of Universal Jobmatch, which facilitates computerised matching and alerts of vacancies in particular fields where jobs are sought for jobseekers. Universal Jobmatch is indicative of a wider trend towards greater reliance on information and communications technology in searching for a job as well as the provision of information, advice and guidance.

Interviewees and participants in the local case study areas expressed concerns about "patchy" provision of careers information and advice in schools and also for adults. In a context of institutional change such a situation was described as a "perfect storm" as young people, their parents and employers faced a diversity of educational institutions and training providers as well as routes to qualifications (academic and vocational) with poor careers guidance and advice. However, the Mansfield Learning Partnership demonstrates how schools, the local authority and employers can come together to create meaningful pathways into education and employment. There is scope to further promote such good practice to see how it can be replicated and adapted elsewhere in England. A key feature of the Mansfield Learning Partnership is the involvement of employers in the education system and in provision and awareness of employers' requirements and local employment opportunities. Recognising employers for their pledges was considered a positive way of highlighting employer engagement in education. The activities of Hull University also provide an example of matching people with higher-level skills to local job opportunities as a means of supporting local economic growth.

In other OECD countries, efforts are being undertaken to better link the education system to employers and to provide youth and adults with good careers advice and progression opportunities. The education system needs to work more closely with the employment and skills system to create clearer, simpler and more recognised pathways into vocational education and training. Career pathway approaches can be used to support young people moving into more vocationally specific careers and set out how this can be done by articulating the knowledge, skills and competencies to better connect education with work in an occupation. In England, there is scope to better trace career pathways into employment-intensive domestic sectors that have high-growth potential and in establishing career clusters (see Box 4.4).

Box 4.4. **Establishing Career Clusters to better connect education and work**

In the United States, the States' Career Clusters Initiative (SCCI) was started about 10 years ago to help states and schools refocus their programmes of career and technical education (CTE) (formerly known as vocational education) around clusters of similar occupations. Traditional vocational education prepared learners with a narrow set of specific skills for certain jobs. That preparation was no longer adequate for workers to remain competitive in a global economy having a changing and dynamic labor market where over a lifetime workers will have multiple careers.

Career clusters and their associated curriculum frameworks integrate both the academic knowledge and technical skills needed for a wide range of occupations, allowing school graduates to pursue career opportunities from entry level through management and professional levels. The objectives of the SCCI are to increase:

- Students' awareness of career options to improve their educational and work choices;
- Students' understanding of the structure and function of businesses so they can be more productive workers; and
- Students' achievement by setting high standards and expectations and teaching academics in a context that interests and motivates learners

The career clusters and their curriculum frameworks reflect the higher academic standards that states have created for preparing more secondary learners for postsecondary education (college-ready) as well as for entry into the labor force (work-ready). They also focus on all aspects of an industry or cluster so that a learner gets exposed to a range of possible occupations and industry standards.

Box 4.4. **Establishing Career Clusters to better connect education and work** *(continued)*

Under the sponsorship of the U.S. Department of Education and the National Association of State Directors of Career/Technical Education, using national advisory committees composed of educators as well as business and industry representatives, the SCCI developed 16 clusters encompassing the 970 or so occupations described by the U.S. Department of Labor's standard occupational codes (SOC). Within the 16 clusters, the SCCI identified 79 career pathways or groupings of similar occupations. Associated with each pathway are programmes of study (sometimes called plans of study) integrating challenging academic content and technical material in a coherent sequence of courses aligning secondary and postsecondary education programmes and resulting in an industry-recognised credential or postsecondary certificate or degree.

Each programme of study rests on standards in the form of a set of knowledge and skill statements. These standards include foundation academic expectations, essential knowledge and skills for work, career cluster knowledge and skills, and career pathway knowledge and skills. In some States (e.g. Florida and South Carolina), secondary learners are expected to choose a career major programme within a career pathway to organise their schooling, while in other States students may elect to do so.

State and local education districts vary in the degree to which they organise their career and technical education programmes around career clusters. Some States use all 16 clusters, while others use fewer or none. States and their local education districts also vary in the career pathways and programmes of study they offer, often depending upon local business and industry needs.

Source: Hamilton, V. (2012), *Career Pathway and Cluster Skill Development: Promising Models from the United States*, OECD Local Economic and Employment Development (LEED) Working Papers, No. 2012/14, OECD Publishing, Paris, http://dx.doi.org/10.1787/5k94g1s6f7td-en.

Targeting policy to local employment sectors and investing in quality jobs

Recommendation: Create more and better jobs by supporting key sectors locally and associated skills development initiatives

The local case studies showed that the Local Enterprise Partnerships and local partners were focusing attention on the identification of key local employment sectors and addressing future skills needs. Particular attention is being focused on those sectors which are likely to generate future value locally and nationally and it is recommended that, in line with the Witty Review, such spatial approaches are used where it makes sectoral sense. However, it is important that those sectors that are significant in terms of volumes of local employment provided are not overlooked. Industrial strategy is forming in key sectors, with business, government and trade unions working together to establish growth. The Government is seeking strategic dialogue about long-term investment priorities through industrial councils and partnerships. Industrial strategy is forming in key sectors Going forward, there is a need to support innovative initiatives seeking to support skills development in strategic sectors (as in the case of Employer First and the low carbon sector) and to learn from them "what works".

It is also salient to note that in the case of Hull the major inward investment of Siemens in offshore green energy technologies was highlighting the fundamental need to ensure that provision for supply of workers with core engineering skills was in place, since the employer could "top up" with specialist training to meet more specific sectoral needs.

In other OECD countries, partnerships and governance networks are being used to develop strategic local sectors, which have a strong potential for economic growth. In the aftermath of the global financial crisis, local areas may benefit from place-based initiatives to promote sectors where they have comparative advantage, while continuing to promote broader economic diversity. Local policy makers often seek to promote "flexible specialisation" – concentrating on certain sectors, but evolving these in response to local and global change. Focusing on local sectors of importance can galvanise public action as well as public-private partnerships around a common interest. England could examine the applicability of recent initiatives in the Unites States and Korea to promote skills development opportunities within certain sectors (see Box 4.5).

Box 4.5. **Sector strategies in the United States and Korea**

Advanced Manufacturing Jobs and Innovation Accelerator Challenge in the United States: Federal economic development policy has embraced the idea of fostering "industry clusters" as a mechanism for driving regional economic growth. Industry clusters represent dense formal and informal networks of companies, a supportive ecosystem for innovation, and deep pools of specialised and skilled workers. Through a series of challenge grant programmes – the Jobs and Innovation Accelerator Challenge grants – the Obama Administration has invested in numerous regional efforts to strengthen and grow regionally-based industry clusters. The challenge grants leverage funding and technical assistance from multiple Federal agencies in a co-ordinated regional effort to generate greater impact than any individual agency might be able to achieve through their respective individual grant programmes.

Although the AMJIAC grants have a complex structure, they do allow flexibility for regions to determine the best way to grow their target clusters and support small and medium-sized manufacturers. Each region draws upon unique assets and capabilities, so regions have chosen their own avenues for achieving this objective. For example, Michigan's "InnoState" AMJIAC project is unique in that it seeks to promote new product manufacturing capability within their existing contract manufacturing firms. This is a collaborative effort among the Michigan Manufacturing Technology Center (MMTC), the National Center for Manufacturing Sciences (NCMS), the Detroit Regional Chamber Foundation, and the Workforce Intelligence Network. The work involves providing opportunities for these existing contract manufacturers to create new products. Working through the Pure Michigan Business Connect Site, the Michigan team provides marketing and other tools for outreach and branding, as well as preparing the manufacturers with lean operations in order to produce products of their own.

Sector strategies in Korea: In Korea, comprehensive strategies have been developed which seek to exploit the opportunities available by fostering growth in locally competitive industries. Bucheon (which is city located just outside of Seoul) has identified moulding, packaging, lighting, robotics, and animation as five strategic growth sectors going forward. These industries were chosen based upon industrial distribution, competitiveness, and future growth in order to transform the existing industrial structure and move to high value added industries that will lead growth into the future.

The city's growth strategy has also identified the importance of attracting firms through industrial clusters that exists in the region. For example, in the lighting sector, companies such as Samsung and LG, are located in the city along with other SMEs, which are important for attracting foreign investment and building new growth. The city has emphasised the importance of intensifying research and development around these clusters through strengthening linkages between industry and education institutions.

Sources: National Institute of Standards and Technology (2013), *The Advanced Manufacturing Jobs and Innovation Accelerator Challenge (AMJIAC) – Mid-Project Review*, Department of Commerce, Washington, DC, http://nist.gov/mep/upload/AMJIAC-Report-final0520.pdf (accessed 24 July 2014); OECD (2014b), Employment and Skills Strategies in Korea, OECD Reviews on Local Job Creation, OECD Publishing, Paris, http://dx.doi.org/10.1787/9789264216563-en.

Recommendation: Focus on the benefits of "decent work" and in-work progression by ensuring that public sector organisations "lead by example" and promoting the business and other benefits (e.g. in terms of reduced costs associated with recruitment and retention) of being a "good employer"

Fostering in-work progression did not emerge as a major focus for activity in the local case study areas; rather the emphasis was on generating jobs (e.g. job quantity rather than job quality). In large measure, this may be a function of public funding being focused on pre-employment and employment entry initiatives, rather than what happens once an individual is employed. However, as the economy continues to grow and skills deficiencies are becoming more apparent, and with the roll out of Universal Credit, there is a key "window of opportunity" in the short-term in England to drive forward the "job quality" and "in-work progression" agenda. There needs to be more policy and analytical focus on in-work progression, including pilots, demonstration projects and trials to gather a robust evidence base on the incentives and support structures that are needed to promote in-work advancement.

A greater emphasis on in-work progression need not be at the expense of getting people into work, as demonstrated by the work programme of the "More Jobs, Better Jobs" Partnership in Leeds between Leeds City Council, Leeds City Region and the Joseph Rowntree Foundation (see Box 4.6). It will be important to learn the lessons from action research conducted by this partnership, including on the role of anchor institutions (e.g. hospitals, universities and major employers in the private sector) in linking poor people to jobs and in tackling in-work poverty, and how to use major capital development/ infrastructure projects to provide employment and training opportunities for local people and enhance the local skills base. Learning the lessons from the experience of the implementation of local living wages (as implemented by some employers in Hull and other cities in the UK) is also important.

Box 4.6. **More Jobs, Better Jobs Partnership in Leeds**

The Joseph Rowntree Foundation (a social research policy charity in the UK funding research on issues of poverty and place) has formed a partnership with Leeds City Council and Leeds City Region to understand why some people and some parts of cities do not share in prosperity and jobs that economic growth can bring and what can be done to change it. The context for activity is that across the Leeds City Region there are projected to be over half a million job opportunities by 2020, but there are 187 thousand workless households. The partnership has been given the name "More jobs, better jobs" in recognition that the quality of jobs matters as much as the number of jobs. The partnership is commissioning evidence reviews and practical research that can shape policy and services in the Leeds area, and share findings with other cities, specifically in relation to how to make addressing poverty and integral part of local growth strategies.

The University of Hull, for example, has an explicit strategic objective to establish itself as an "anchor institution" for the Hull and Humber region. As the only higher education institution in the sub-region (as compared with two in Nottingham/North Nottinghamshire), the University sees itself as being in a good position to play a leading role in a number of aspects of the local economy and society (University of Hull, 2011):

> As an anchor institution the University of Hull will ensure that its local and regional communities benefit by its presence and local interaction, just as the University

> benefits by its geographical location and engagement with its communities... As an anchor institution, the University of Hull will be a symbol of aspiration and inspiration, hope, pride and confidence to its local communities. It can best achieve this by being a university that participates in the international as well as national and regional arenas on the highest levels of academic excellence and scholarship.

This extract from the University's Strategic Plan demonstrates that the concept of an "anchor institution" can be broader than demonstrating good practice in employment, skills and related issues. An anchor institution can be symbolic for areas such as Hull, providing a link to international good practice

The UK Commission's "ladder of opportunity" framework – *(1)* Getting in; *(2)* Getting on; *(3)* Moving up – is useful for conceptualising and planning how working with employers and promoting skills development activities which can support sectoral and local economic development priorities (see Box 4.7) (UK Commission for Employment and Skills, 2014a).

Box 4.7. **Challenges and associated policy initiatives across the "Ladder of Opportunity"**

	Challenges	*Policy initiatives*
Getting in: bottom rung	• Getting into work • Getting beyond precarious, short-term work	• Improving education and qualifications • Integration of work experience into study programmes to create robust career pathways into work
Getting on: middle rung	• Progressing through the middle rungs on the "Ladder of Opportunity" in the context of contraction of space on such rungs with the contraction of clerical and blue-collar jobs with the development of an "hourglass economy"	• Improving and disseminating intelligence to inform lifelong career decision-making • Creating robust career pathways through the middle rungs (e.g. via Apprenticeships)
Moving up: top rung	• Improving skills utilisation of top talent to enhance innovation and value added	• Education and training for higher level skills – informed by (local) sectoral needs • Exploitation of work based routes to higher skilled jobs • Promotion of high performance working

There is scope for exploring how funding mechanisms for employment and skills initiatives might be adjusted to place greater emphasis of earnings and progression in employment (i.e. moving a step further ahead of the "payment by results" model in the Work Programme that rewards employment retention). In "Growth Through People" the UK Commission for Employment and Skills (2014b) emphasised the links between skills, employment prospects, pay, well-being and business competitiveness, and noted set out as a priority for action: "improving workplace productivity should be recognised as the key route to increasing pay and prosperity". There is a case for changing incentive structures so that training providers and employer ownership of skills consortia are incentivised to tackle work organisation and management issues. Backed by appropriate funding, universities could be encouraged/incentivised to undertake applied research of relevance to stimulating productivity in local strategic sectors and then transfer such knowledge freely where needed. There is also scope for employers to take action on these issues and promote themselves as "good employers"/"employers of choice" without additional financial incentives.

Ensuring employment and in-work progression is a key aspect of job quality. OECD research has shown that low-skilled adults are generally less likely to access training and this situation is often exacerbated for individuals who lack contact with local labour markets through long term and sometimes multigenerational unemployment. Many communities are faced with the need to respond to a "stagnation of participation" in education and training amongst the lower skilled. Lower-skilled people are increasingly employed on a temporary basis, with it being unusual now for such workers to gain a "career for life", and it can be difficult to see how one job may lead to another higher up within the job hierarchy. Putting in place the right policy mechanisms for employment progression can support low-skilled employees in particular to advance in a given occupation or sector.

Box 4.8. **Supporting in-work progression in the United States and Australia**

Career Pathways for Frontline Health Care Workers in the United States: *Jobs to Careers: Transforming the Front Lines of Health Care Workers* is an initiative to test the effectiveness of a career pathways approach for clerical, technical, and direct service workers in 17 sites across the United States. It is sponsored by the Robert Wood Johnson Foundation in collaboration with the Hitachi Foundation and the U.S. Department of Labor.

Frontline healthcare workers in the United States are predominantly female and disproportionally ethnic minorities. They often have low levels of educational achievement and generally receive low wages and poor training. A number of barriers hinder upskilling and career progression, including lack of education, lack of knowledge of how to navigate the education system, limited time for training and lack of employer support.

To help overcome these barriers, partnerships were created between health care employers and educational institutions in the 17 Jobs to Career programme sites. These partnerships used a career pathways approach that created defined "rungs" on a career ladder from entry level to more advanced positions, each with a corresponding set of credentials and skills. These pathways helped workers either advance within occupations, or between occupations, or transcend professional scope.

Research on 6 of the 17 sites identified a number of promising strategies. First, programmes should be designed with employer needs in mind – for example where there are vacancies or in high growth jobs. Based on these desired objectives, mapping career ladders, identifying any missing steps between rungs, and identifying the competencies and credentials needed at each level is essential. Additionally, career pathways programmes must be designed in a way that aligns the needs and customs of educational institutions and workplaces, including modifying curricula as needed and integrating work-based learning opportunities. Attention must also be paid to formal systems and organisational cultures, as shifts in these can be critical to project success. Incentives and rewards should be structured in a way to make the programmer attractive to workers. Both monetary (e.g. pay raises) and non-monetary awards (e.g. enhanced feelings of self-worth) can incentivise participation. Participant recruitment can be achieved through a variety of means, including marketing directly to eligible employers and asking supervisors for recommendations. Finally, a team effort is needed for project management and monitoring.

Box 4.8. **Supporting in-work progression in the United States and Australia** *(continued)*

Local company in Australia re-skilling their employees to open the door to opportunities: Dexion puts its success down to initiatives to help better harness the skills, expertise and ideas of its employees, 50% of whom have been with the company for more than 10 years. These initiatives include introducing new strategies to boost information sharing and employee participation in decision making. Other strategies such as multi-skilling, job rotation, mentoring, a "buddy" system, skills planning and training opportunities have also increased the ability of staff to utilise their skills. Dexion uses a skills matrix to determine its skill needs to meet operational requirements. The skills matrix aligns operators (workers) with the tasks required for each business unit. The matrix has a grading system that identifies whether staff are: trainee, competent or expert. The Manufacturing Co-ordinator and Team Leader identify the skills needs of the team and a review of the skills matrix takes place regularly. Planning is undertaken on a monthly basis and considers past needs and future needs depending on the requirements from the supply chain.

Since 2009, Dexion has teamed up with Western Sydney Institute of TAFE to offer a Certificate III in Competitive Manufacturing, tailored to suit the needs of the business. All staff were offered the opportunity to participate in training, with training for team leaders available at Certificate IV. Training occurred on-site, with training aligned to the shift patterns. Participants were placed in crossfunctional teams which undertook practical projects to identify improvement initiatives in all units of the industrial component of the business.

Sources: Skills Australia (2012), *Better Use of Skills, Better Outcomes: A Research Report on Skills Utilisation in Australia*, Commonwealth of Australia, Canberra, www.awpa.gov.au/publications/documents/Skills-utilisation-research-report-15-May-2012.pdf, (accessed 18 July 2014); Zacker, H. B. (n.d.), *Creating Career Pathways for Frontline Health Care Workers*, Jobs for the Future, Washington, DC, www.jff.org/publications/creating-career-pathways-frontline-health-care-workers, (accessed 15 July 2014).

Recommendation: Develop policies, which encourage the better utilisation of skills and examine the role that Universities and Further Education colleges can play in this area

A key pillar of job quality is better utilising the skills of those already at work. This requires not only considering how skills are provided by the education and training system, but the extent to which employers develop and utilise skills in the production process. OECD research has shown that local public agencies can contribute to improving how skills are put to use by using a number of different policy instruments, such as incentives for employers to invest in new technology and the promotion of more effective forms of work organisation (Froy and Giguère, 2010). In many countries, it can be difficult for the public sector to advise business on productivity issues, as there is a "credibility" gap which needs to be filled before policy makers can successfully get involved in this area. To overcome this, it can help to work with intermediaries, such as vocational education institutions or other third party organisations, which specialise in these activities.

Management practices are important here, as new ideas are more likely to emerge when workers have the ability to use their discretion and "learn by doing". This applies both to workers involved in production, and workers directly dealing with and responding to customer needs (Froy and Giguère, 2010). Equally important is the ability of the company or organisation to recognise and mainstream such new ideas and approaches across the workforce as a whole (Toner, 2011).

Skills demand and utilisation will increase if existing firms are able to diversify, upgrade their product market strategies and move towards more knowledge-intensive production processes. As companies move into higher value added product and service markets, the levels of skills that they require, and the extent to which they utilise skills, tends to increase. Of course, the ability of firms to move towards higher-value added product market sectors will depend on access to appropriate markets. Strategies to upgrade product market strategies need to be accompanied by strategies to build local markets and better access regional, national and international markets.

Non-technological innovation can also emerge from within firms, particularly when the skills of their workers are well-utilised. Innovative new ideas often come from problem-solving on the "shop floor" or in front line services, and the importance of incremental innovation has been underlined in the OECD's Innovation Strategy (OECD, 2010).

Universities and further education colleges can be instrumental in helping local industries to better access and better utilise skills when they are fully embedded in local economies. In areas of traditional low-skills, low-wage employment, the role played by vocational training colleges in stimulating innovation in the local economy would seem to be particularly important. However in order for them to be involved, it is important that funding streams and performance management targets reward and encourage this type of "locally embedded" activity.

To carry out this work, engagement in meaningful and strategic partnerships will be key. Local collaboration is needed between policy makers in the spheres of economic development, education and employment, in order to ensure that skills policies are understood in the context of broader economic development. Such collaboration can be both formal and informal, strategic and operational.

In Flanders, Belgium, collaborations have been built between the unions, academics and government representatives to help managers to promote better skills utilisation in a number of different sectors. Such collaboration is particularly in evidence in the province of Limburg. The fragility of the local economy, which has traditionally been based on low-skilled work and a few major employers, was recently demonstrated by the movement of a major employer, Ford, out of the region. Local policy makers are now faced with the problem of finding new employment for low skilled ex-factory workers whose transferable skills are limited. At the same time, there is a desire to move the region towards more productive higher skilled employment. The local ACV union has responded by setting up practice labs for innovative work organisation, in co-operation with a coalition between academics, unions, enterprises and consultants (Flanders Synergy), subsidised by the Flemish government (see Box 4.9).

The Foundation for Innovation in Work (*Stichting Innovatie en Arbeid)* in Flanders also collects examples of initiatives that combine skills utilisation and work organisation, making these tools publicly available through a website (OECD, 2014c). The health and social care sectors in Flanders have also been the focus of restructuring to produce better quality jobs in a number of regions, spurred on by local labour and skills shortages. In Limburg, the Provincial Development Agency (POM Limburg) set up a platform to address work organisation issues within the care sector in 2010 called *Platform Zorglandschap Limburg* (Platform Care Limburg), with support from the provincial government. This scheme has focused on improving work organisation within local hospitals and nursing homes to create more flexible work organisation and increase labour productivity. One workstream has focused on combining part-time jobs across organisations to create full-time jobs (OECD, 2014c). This shows the potential for the public sector to improve skills utilisation and job quality in its own workforce, which can be particularly important in rural areas where the public sector is a significant local employer.

Box 4.9. **Practice labs for innovative work organisation, Flanders, Belgium**

In Limburg in Flanders, "Practice labs for innovative work organisation" have been set up to work with businesses on work organisation issues. The ACV union has played a key role in establishing and implementing the initiative.

The practice labs have been set up in the construction, logistics, healthcare, social economy, social service/care sector and agricultural sectors. Separate labs were established for each sector but in practice, labs can work with mixed groups, and can support both large and small firms. Eight workshops have taken place in 2013/14, each involving 6-8 companies. A consultant was hired to work on the workshops. They function as a learning network where companies share experience. Managers are encouraged to consider where they can effect change to make sure that workers have more involvement in the way that the firm operates.

Each lab covers seven themes, each of which is a different area where the manager can have an influence. One theme, for example, has been exploring new ways that firms can expand their market base to improve the quality of their organisation (in terms of efficiency, flexibility, quality, innovation, sustainability) while also improving job quality. Supervisors play the role of coach and act as a sounding board for participants who have questions, both within and outside of the lab sessions. Participants receive assignments to translate theory into practice when they return to the workplace. Unions report that the workshops have improved their relationships with local employers. The workshops have proved so useful that one sector, construction, is now running its own labs, independent of public funding.

Source: OECD (2015, forthcoming), *Employment and Skills Strategies in Flanders, Belgium*, OECD Reviews on Local Job Creation, OECD Publishing, Paris, http://dx.doi.org/10.1787/9789264228740-en.

Recommendation: Continue to promote and support entrepreneurship initiatives

Promotion of entrepreneurship was widely recognised as an important area for development, at all levels from primary school to university. There was some evidence of success with localised initiatives at schools in Hull. However, there was general agreement that there is a long way to go to close the entrepreneurship gap between prosperous and less prosperous areas. At the higher education levels in Nottingham, there was evidence that specialist entrepreneurship support activities (as provided by the Hive) could be beneficial. While many aspects of entrepreneurship support are generic, it is also clear that delivery should also take account of context and the needs of different local areas, and be mindful of whether entrepreneurship represented a "real opportunity" or was really a "last resort" when individuals' attempts to gain a position failed.

Within many OECD countries, a lack of entrepreneurship skills is often cited as one of the most significant barriers to business creation and self-employment and frequently contributes to difficulties in accessing financing. Entrepreneurial capabilities and competences can be supported and nurtured through education and training. It is also important that the government in England re-examines the role of entrepreneurship training within vocational training, including examining the way that vocational schools interact with industry. Current entrepreneurship education in vocational training emphasises formal business plans and while this is important, the focus should be on the "how to" element (OECD, 2014d).

Entrepreneurship skills can also be developed outside of the education system. The advantages of entrepreneurship training outside of formal education are that it can be targeted at business owners and potential business owners, and reach people who are not in formal education. It can also focus more on practical entrepreneurship skills than formal education courses, which are as much about generating entrepreneurial mind sets as they are about imparting entrepreneurship skills to people with start-up intentions or existing businesses. It is also relatively easy to design and/or deliver entrepreneurship training courses to particular communities of disadvantaged or under-represented people in entrepreneurship (see Box 4.10).

Box 4.10. **Fostering local economic development through the promotion of entrepreneurship**

Entrepreneurial activity is seen as one of the keys to diversifying the local economy of Shawinigan, Canada. For many years, Shawinigan was an industrial town built around its large electric power facility and heavy industry. Industrialisation brought steady well-paying work in forestry, aluminium production and textiles. The city became a victim of structural changes in the global economy with many employers shutting down their operations. With the impending closure of another enterprise in 2009, prominent people in the community were brought together to look at the future of city considering its strengths and weaknesses. Based on this collaboration, the city is pursuing an approach that looks to develop a community of entrepreneurs and small business operations as a sustainable economic base.

What is of particular interesting about this approach is the partnership of a number of different actors each guided by a different policy focus (e.g. economic development, education or employment) to implement a local horizontal approach. The mechanism for this integration was a small amount of funding directed to the municipality by a departing employer. A Diversification Committee was established composed of key funding and government agencies. The committee realised that in order to be effective, they would have to create a common local plan that would inform their vertical accountabilities. Specific areas of collaboration have been the strategic use of non-governmental and governmental funding to maximise total grants. An entrepreneurial forum was created to:

- Promote entrepreneurism as a career;
- Increase the percentage of individuals choosing an entrepreneurial path;
- Develop entrepreneurial attributes among the youth;
- Grow synergies among organisations that develop the economy and community; and,
- Recognise and emphasise initiative, creativity, solidarity and communal engagement

In collaboration with the school commission, Shawinigan opened the entrepreneurship centre in 2013. The entrepreneurship centre is located in an old textile factory which has been completely renovated. The city of Shawinigan advanced USD 3 million for the project with approximately USD 2 million coming from other sources. The entrepreneurship centre offers skills development programmes along with other supports that will allow the growth of a critical mass of entrepreneurs. Future entrepreneurs will be supported over a 5 year period: The first 18 months focused on training and start-up; The second 18 months will be dedicated to management and operations within space provided in the Centre; and The final two years will be given to consolidating the operations of the new enterprise and its relocation into the community.

Source: OECD (2014e), *Employment and Skills Strategies in Canada*, OECD Reviews on Local Job Creation, OECD Publishing, Paris, http://dx.doi.org/10.1787/9789264209374-en.

Inclusion

Recommendation: Continue to target employment and skills programmes to at-risk youth and other disadvantaged groups to develop their employability skills and better connect them with the labour market. Make greater use of voluntary/community and private sector actors.

In England employment and training policies place a strong emphasis on the disadvantaged. In recent years, a key focus of activity has been on tackling youth unemployment, specifically NEETs, and this was evident in the local case study areas. While the economic crisis has touched all young people, some groups face particular challenges. Youth not in employment, education or training (i.e. NEETs) face the greatest barriers in entering the labour market. This group requires the most immediate attention from policy makers because they are at risk of withdrawing from the labour market and never returning. Some indications of success were apparent in targeting NEET policies and attempting a range of different interventions, including an emphasis on co-creation – with young people playing a major role in the design of interventions in the Talent Match programme which started in 2014 in 21 local areas in England (including Hull and Nottingham). However, with a multiplicity of initiatives, there were concerns that the different initiatives and organisations were "tripping over each other".

There was general agreement that the voluntary and community sector had an important role to play in outreach to engage the most disadvantaged young people and to help them make initial steps on a pathway towards employment. There was also recognition of the important role of providing information on careers, and of advice and guidance, and concern that this was not available equally to all. Likewise there was a widespread view that work experience can play an important role in helping young people appreciate what employment entails and the attributes and skills employers are looking for, while also providing insights for employers into the contribution young people can make to their businesses.

It is also important that there is continued investment in early years education and support for those who are falling behind at school. This is necessary to help tackle ongoing inequalities in life chances and address shortfalls in social mobility which are particularly stark in England, where socio-economic background is particularly important in determining skills outcomes compared with many other OECD countries. In turn, such outcomes influence the long-term employability and adaptability of the labour force.

Apprenticeships and VET programmes have a role to play here in reducing and offsetting educational inequalities. An approach that views youth as "problems to be solved" by a single public agency is unlikely to be effective. Rather, public employment services, schools and training institutions need to come together to create the community conditions in which children and youth are more likely to succeed. This is best achieved through programmes that are grounded in the local context and have a commitment from partners to align resources, co-ordinate programmes and policies, and engage in a high level of communication and data sharing. The Plug-in project in Sweden provides good example of a local project, which targets disadvantaged youth who have not completed upper secondary school (see Box 4.11).

Box 4.11. **Plug in: A Collaborative Project to Improve the Completion Rate in Swedish Upper Secondary Schools**

Plug In is a Sweden-wide project to reduce by half the proportion of students who do not complete upper secondary school in four years – from 24% to 12%. The project operates at a number of levels. The Swedish Association of Local Authorities and Regions (SALAR), which represents the governmental, professional and employer-related interests of Sweden's municipalities and county councils, plays the lead national co-ordination role. SALAR's five participating regional councils translate the national objectives to the regional level, promote regional collaboration, and support the work of schools and municipalities. Finally, local, municipal, and/or school authorities are responsible for implementing the more than 100 initiatives and projects that comprise Plug In. The European Social Fund provides funding for the project, which is matched by the local municipalities.

Because of the decentralised nature of the project, there is no single Plug In model. Rather, regions, municipalities, and schools have taken various approaches. Some projects focus on improving processes and systems – for example, improving the transfer information about at-risk students when they start upper secondary school and improving IT systems to track students across schools. Other projects focus more on support to students, such as enhanced outreach to students who have dropped out or are at risk of dropping out, individualised coaching and mentoring, and study support.

For example, the Gothenburg region has a regional focus on expanding on municipalities' legal mandate to stay informed about people aged 16 to 20 who are not in upper secondary school. The project supports municipalities in moving beyond just tracking these young people to active engagement. Through municipal re-engagement centres or hubs, multi-skilled teams work with these young people to help them identify positive next steps in their lives. In addition to this region-wide focus, individual municipalities and schools have also developed their own individual projects, many of which complement existing support measures. One municipality in the region, Kungsbacka, has developed a comprehensive approach, having implemented projects that provide individualised additional support, flexible modes of learning, and support to students with mental health issues. It is also tackling non-completion in adult education colleges.

In the Västerbotten region, most of the seven participating municipalities are using "First Rooms" to provide individualised support to students with high rates of absence, those who have left school before completion, and those facing other barriers. First Rooms are full-time, but temporary programmes, that use an approach grounded in cognitive behavioural therapy to motivate students to return to their studies. They also offer study support and link students with other specialised supports. While this general model is common amongst most of the municipalities in the region, each implements it slightly differently. For example, in the only larger municipality in the region, Umeå, the First Room draws students from several schools and has its own separate location. In one of the small and remote municipalities in the region, one of the activities of the First Room is fishing. This activity takes advantage of the municipalities' rural location and gives the sole staff member of the First Room the opportunity to build relationships with the students and promote group cohesion.

Nationally, Plug In includes an explicit focus on collecting and disseminating knowledge and information about strategies to address the dropout problem. PlugInnovation, an online knowledge sharing platform, was developed specifically for this purpose. However, because most of Plug In's interventions started in 2013, it is too early to determine the success of the various interventions being implemented locally and regionally. A number of evaluations are underway, including an internal evaluation of ten selected projects and two external evaluations (an outcomes-focused evaluation and a process-focused evaluation).

Source: Stromback, T. (2015, forthcoming), *Plug In: A Collaborative Project to Improve the Completion Rate in Swedish Upper Secondary Schools*, prepared for 10th Annual Meeting of the Forum on Partnerships and Local Governance, OECD Publishing, Paris.

References

Giguère, S. and F. Froy (eds.) (2009), *Flexible Policy for More and Better Jobs*, Local Economic and Employment Development (LEED), OECD Publishing, Paris, http://dx.doi.org/10.1787/9789264059528-en.

Hamilton, V. (2012), "Career Pathway and Cluster Skill Development: Promising Models from the United States", *OECD Local Economic and Employment Development (LEED) Working Papers*, No. 2012/14, OECD Publishing, Paris, http://dx.doi.org/10.1787/5k94g1s6f7td-en.

National Institute of Standards and Technology (2013), *The Advanced Manufacturing Jobs and Innovation Accelerator Challenge (AMJIAC) – Mid-Project Review*, Department of Commerce, Washington, DC, http://nist.gov/mep/upload/AMJIAC-Report-final0520.pdf (accessed 24 July 2014).

OECD (2015, forthcoming) *Employment and Skills Strategies in Flanders*, Belgium, OECD Reviews on Local Job Creation, OECD Publishing, Paris, http://dx.doi.org/10.1787/9789264228740-en.

OECD (2014a), *Connecting People with Jobs: Activation Policies in the United Kingdom*, OECD Publishing, Paris, http://dx.doi.org/10.1787/9789264217188-en.

OECD (2014b), *Employment and Skills Strategies in Korea*, OECD Reviews on Local Job Creation, OECD Publishing, Paris, http://dx.doi.org/10.1787/9789264216563-en.

OECD (2014c), *Job Creation and Local Economic Development*, OECD Publishing, Paris, http://dx.doi.org/10.1787/9789264215009-en.

OECD (2014d), *Supporting Graduate Entrepreneurship in Wielkopolska and Kujawsko-Pomorskie, Poland*, OECD, Paris, www.efs.gov.pl/analizyraportypodsumowania/documents/graduate_entrepreneurship_in_poland.pdf.

OECD (2014e), *Employment and Skills Strategies in Canada*, OECD Reviews on Local Job Creation, OECD Publishing, Paris, http://dx.doi.org/10.1787/9789264209374-en.

Skills Australia (2012), *Better Use of Skills, Better Outcomes: A Research Report on Skills Utilisation in Australia*, Commonwealth of Australia, Canberra, www.awpa.gov.au/publications/documents/Skills-utilisation-research-report-15-May-2012.pdf (accessed 18 July 2014).

Stromback, Thorsten (2015, forthcoming). *Plug In: A Collaborative Project to Improve the Completion Rate in Swedish Upper Secondary Schools.* Prepared for 10th Annual Meeting of the Forum on Partnerships and Local Governance, OECD Publishing, Paris.

UK Commission for Employment and Skills (2014a), *Climbing the ladder: skills for sustainable recovery*, UKCES, Wath-upon-Dearne and London, https://www.gov.uk/government/uploads/system/uploads/attachment_data/file/378968/Summer_What_0v41.pdf (accessed 18 July 2014).

UK Commission for Employment and Skills (2014b), *Growth Through People*, UKCES, Wath-upon-Dearne and London, https://www.gov.uk/government/uploads/system/uploads/attachment_data/file/378810/14.11.26._GTP_V18.3_FINAL_FOR_WEB.pdf (accessed 18 July 2014).

University of Hull (2013), *Strategic Plan 2011-2015*, University of Hull, Hull, http://www2.hull.ac.uk/hideplan/strategic_plan/4_an_engaged_university.aspx, (accessed 18 July 2014).

Zacker, H. B. (n.d.), *Creating Career Pathways for Frontline Health Care Workers*, Jobs for the Future, Washington, DC, http://www.jff.org/publications/creating-career-pathways-frontline-health-care-workers (accessed 15 July 2014).

ORGANISATION FOR ECONOMIC CO-OPERATION AND DEVELOPMENT

The OECD is a unique forum where governments work together to address the economic, social and environmental challenges of globalisation. The OECD is also at the forefront of efforts to understand and to help governments respond to new developments and concerns, such as corporate governance, the information economy and the challenges of an ageing population. The Organisation provides a setting where governments can compare policy experiences, seek answers to common problems, identify good practice and work to co-ordinate domestic and international policies.

The OECD member countries are: Australia, Austria, Belgium, Canada, Chile, the Czech Republic, Denmark, Estonia, Finland, France, Germany, Greece, Hungary, Iceland, Ireland, Israel, Italy, Japan, Korea, Luxembourg, Mexico, the Netherlands, New Zealand, Norway, Poland, Portugal, the Slovak Republic, Slovenia, Spain, Sweden, Switzerland, Turkey, the United Kingdom and the United States. The European Commission takes part in the work of the OECD.

OECD Publishing disseminates widely the results of the Organisation's statistics gathering and research on economic, social and environmental issues, as well as the conventions, guidelines and standards agreed by its members.

LOCAL ECONOMIC AND EMPLOYMENT DEVELOPMENT (LEED)

The OECD Programme on Local Economic and Employment Development (LEED) has advised governments and communities since 1982 on how to respond to economic change and tackle complex problems in a fast-changing world. Its mission is to contribute to the creation of more and better quality jobs through more effective policy implementation, innovative practices, stronger capacities and integrated strategies at the local level. LEED draws on a comparative analysis of experience from the five continents in fostering economic growth, employment and inclusion. For more information on the LEED Programme, please visit *www.oecd.org/cfe/leed*.

OECD PUBLISHING, 2, rue André-Pascal, 75775 PARIS CEDEX 16
(84 2015 04 1 P) ISBN 978-92-64-22806-1 – No. 61107 2013

www.ingramcontent.com/pod-product-compliance
Lightning Source LLC
LaVergne TN
LVHW081413110826
845149LV00010B/1730

* 9 7 8 9 2 6 4 2 2 8 0 6 1 *